MEDIEVAL STORY

MEDIEVAL STORY

and the beginnings of the
social ideals of English-speaking people

WILLIAM   WITHERLE   LAWRENCE

Second Edition

FREDERICK UNGAR PUBLISHING CO.
NEW YORK

TO

BRANDER MATTHEWS

INTERPRETER OF THE LITERATURE AND LIFE

OF MODERN TIMES

PREFACE

In accordance with the terms of the Hewitt Foundation, the following lectures, delivered during the months of February and March, 1911, at Cooper Union in New York City, are herewith issued in book form.

It seems desirable to remind the reader who is unfamiliar with the conditions under which the Hewitt Lectures are given that they are designed, in part at least, for a less academic audience than that usually in attendance upon lectures given under the auspices of Columbia University. In the present instance, no acquaintance with medieval literature, nor, indeed, any interest in it on the part of the audience could be taken for granted. The course was therefore designed primarily to reveal the charm of this literature, and its significance for modern times. With this end in view, such narrative poetry was selected for analysis as would best illustrate a single theme, — the development of social ideals in the history of the English people. The successive lectures were, however, mainly devoted to discussing this early poetry as literature, in the belief that an understanding of its subject-matter, its origins, and its spirit would best lead to a comprehension of its significance as an index of social progress. It should perhaps be stated that while the general outline of each lecture was strictly adhered to in actual delivery before the audience, the manuscript was not closely followed, much of the speaking being extemporaneous.

In preparing the lectures for the press, few changes have been made. The writer feels that the published volume ought to represent the aims of the Foundation, which was not to appeal to a restricted audience of scholars. Consequently this book is designed for the general reader rather than for the specialist. Whenever it has seemed best to emphasize a point familiar to every student, this has been done without hesitation. Illustrative material from other medieval sources than those discussed here has been sparingly introduced, since the unfamiliar is seldom truly illuminating. No space has been devoted to the discussion of disputed questions; the position which appears to the author most reasonable has been adopted without comment. Since the aim of the book is to make medieval literature seem real and vital, the apparatus of scholarship has been discarded; footnotes have been dispensed with so far as possible, and learned citations avoided. The reader who desires further information will find in the appendix directions for more detailed study.

Although the volume is not primarily designed for those who are familiar with the Middle Ages, the writer hopes that they may not find it without interest, as presenting familiar material from a point of view which should make it as significant for the historian and the sociologist as for the student of literature. It is well, too, even for those whose knowledge is most profound, to forget learning occasionally, and to view these old poems as human documents, as the records of the imagination and of the aspiration of our remoter ancestors.

Finally, the writer would express his gratitude for the generous assistance of his colleagues, Professor Harry Morgan Ayres and Professor George Philip Krapp, in

reading manuscript and proof. His greatest debt, however, is to Professor Brander Matthews, to whose friendly
interest and aid is due more than can easily be stated.

WILLIAM WITHERLE LAWRENCE.

MAY 29, 1911.

PREFACE TO THE SECOND EDITION

In issuing a new edition of this book, it seems best to
make no changes in the text. The aim of the original
lectures was to show the significance of medieval literature
for contemporary political and social conditions. Since
1911 the world's attitude towards democracy has been
altered by the consequences of a war which affected every
civilized people on the globe. It would be impossible to
adapt what was written fifteen years ago to conditions of
the present day without a complete rewriting, in particular
of the opening chapter. To those who use the book in
the years to come the meaning of these changes will be
too vivid to need emphasis.

The case is different, however, with the Suggestions for
Supplementary Reading. It has seemed best to revise
this section somewhat, since the book has been considerably used in colleges and universities by those who need
guidance for further study. I should like to emphasize
once more that the bibliography presents only a selection
of some of the material which is likely to prove most
helpful. Many works of importance and interest have of
necessity been omitted.

WILLIAM WITHERLE LAWRENCE.

OCTOBER 1, 1926.

CONTENTS

CONTENTS

I

INTRODUCTION

" Let me make the ballads of a nation,
and who will may make its laws."

I

INTRODUCTION

EARLY in the month of March, 1910, the daily papers of New York City reported that there had just been unusual excitement in the little principality of Monaco. The home of the most famous gambling establishment in the world has always known excitement enough; the sunny skies of Monte Carlo have looked down on many a tragedy of blighted hopes and ruined fortunes. This particular disturbance, however, was of quite another sort, arousing no interest among the hectic figures hanging about the gambling tables in the casino, but affecting the residents of the principality itself. The streets of the capital had been filled with a hurrying crowd, and noisy with the sound of many voices raised in eager discussion. Nearly half of the male population of this little country had marched to the palace, and demanded — a constitution! They had declared, so the account runs, "that Monaco was the only absolute monarchy remaining on the face of the globe," and that the time for a change had come. Their protest was heeded; the prince of Monaco received a deputation from the crowd, and promised to consider its wishes.

This episode, though unimportant in itself, is not without a certain significance. It illustrates the triumph of the democratic theory of government, the conviction of the people that their right to have a voice in the making of the laws may now be considered established, and the recognition of the ruling powers that such a right cannot be denied them. The acceptance of this principle has come about within a comparatively short time. Scarcely more than a century ago, the Empress Catherine the Great of Russia is said to have expressed the belief that kings and queens should be as little disturbed by the cries of the people as the moon is by the baying of dogs. But not much is heard of such views nowadays. Occasionally, it is true, an echo of bygone despotism disturbs the Continent, but the popular answer to such doctrine leaves little doubt as to whence the sovereign's power is really derived. The present Czar of Russia is perhaps the most autocratic monarch in Europe, but he is obliged to mask his absolutism behind a show of constitutional government. He may act in accord with the sentiments of his illustrious predecessor the Empress Catherine, but he would never dream of avowing them himself. The very fact that it is felt necessary in Russia to maintain this pretense is significant of better times and of a changed order of things. The Oriental countries, too, have been deeply affected by liberal ideals in recent years. Persia has for some time been struggling to make constitutional government effective. The recent deposition of Abdul Hamid from the throne of Turkey may well be a warning to Oriental sovereigns who fail to note the dangers of acknowledged despotism. It is a wise ruler who heeds the signs of the times, and this sign is indeed plain for all to see. "The most striking and impressive of all movements of the century," says President Butler, after reminding us how crowded this time has been with epoch-making events, "is the political development toward the form of government known as democracy."

Yet this practically universal acceptance of liberal institutions really settles nothing definitively; it is the victory of an ideal rather than of a practical system. We are everywhere reminded that it is only a phase of the great struggle between aristocracy and democracy, which has been going on for hundreds of years. The sequel to the uprising in Monaco affords an amusing illustration of this; a constitution was indeed granted to the principality, but so ingeniously was this devised that little real benefit was secured to the people. As Dr. Dillon humorously remarks, "Prince Albert discerned with joy that he would have to perform a kind of constitutional egg-dance, to give with one hand and take away with the other." But Monaco is not the only locality in which egg-dances are in vogue. Here in America it has taken us a long time to see that a republic may be as oligarchic as a monarchy, to recognize, as Lowell once said, "that popular government is not in itself a panacea, is no better than any other except as the virtue and wisdom of the people make it so." We live in a country which affords the most conspicuous example of materially successful popular government on the globe, yet democracy is in one sense as much an issue now as it was when the embattled farmers made a stand at the bridge at Concord, and fired the shot heard round the world. Our concern at present is to make the principles for which those men fought effective in the spirit as well as in the letter;

to be sure that we are not forgetting that in a republic every man should have a fair chance, and that no class should enjoy privileges to which it is not justly entitled. We hear this statement on every hand, both from the popular writer and the philosophic thinker. A recent periodical sums up the paramount issues now facing the great political parties as "between Oligarchy and Democracy; between rule by the few and rule by the many," giving as illustrations the management of our colonial possessions, the election of officials through direct primaries, the labor question, the regulation of railways, and the conservation of natural resources. A close student of American politics, Mr. William Garrott Brown, has defined the situation in a similar way. "We are confronted," he says, "with the problem of adapting the democratic principle to conditions that did not exist when our American democracy arose in the world: that is to say, to a field no longer unlimited, to opportunities no longer boundless, and to an industrial order in which competition is no longer the controlling principle, an industrial order which is, therefore, no longer democratic, but increasingly oligarchical, which may even become, in a way, monarchical, dynastic." There must inevitably be many honest differences of opinion as to how far popular government may be administered effectively without putting great power into the hands of a small number of men. Lord Cromer has called attention to the weakness of the Athenian Commonwealth, especially after the death of Pericles, — "the only example the history of the world can show of an absolute democracy — that is to say, of a government in which power was exercised by the people directly, and not through the intermediary of their representatives. The fact that the experiment has never been repeated is in itself an almost sufficient proof that the system, in spite of the very intense and ennobling spirit of patriotism which it certainly engendered, was a complete failure."

Making a democracy effective in practice as well as in theory is of course quite as much a social as a political problem, and of late this broader point of view has been receiving constantly increasing attention. Issues which were formerly considered purely as a part of governmental administration are now frequently examined as ethical problems. The right of the state to exercise control over private business for the good of the public is an admirable illustration of that democracy which is founded upon social sympathy, which insists upon a generous coöperation among the different members of a free state. In this sense the problems of democracy are manifold, and they are occupying the attention of the public now as never before in years. Abuses of privilege are pilloried on every hand ; magazines and newspapers are full of exposures of the misuse of power ; current novels and dramas exhibit the conflicts between generosity and selfishness, between uprightness and knavery, which arise in such a complex social order as ours. Dr. Washington Gladden has recently urged the necessity of a more democratic church, asserting that too small a proportion of the public ministry is devoted to true social service. The issue is clothed in a multitude of forms, but its underlying spirit remains the same.

This awakening of the national conscience is a new thing, the growth of the past few years. Although it has been used to further political ends, it is not the result of agitation; it is an expression of popular sentiment. In times of prosperity a country is likely to lapse into complacency, which makes our present desire to set our house in order all the more striking. Such an awakening is comprehensible enough when it precedes a great struggle; the War of the Rebellion was fought for an ideal of democracy as well as for more material issues, and the Revolution might have been avoided if sentiment could have been sacrificed to expediency. There are those, indeed, who see analogies to such times of upheaval at the present day. A well-known magazine, which is not given to exploiting sensations, publishes an article which aims to show "that the causes of the political and industrial crises through which we are passing to-day are the same as the causes of the most momentous episode of our history, the Civil War." But whatever we may think of the resemblances between the conditions of fifty years ago and those of the present day, we must recognize that the differences are equally striking. Historical parallels are likely to be misleading, not because the events of one age do not find their counterpart in a later time, but because these events are complicated by many other issues, which may apparently be unimportant, but which may really exert a profound and even determining influence upon the ultimate outcome. Decision in regard to such matters is difficult. Modern civilization is too complex a mechanism to yield readily to analysis, and we are too near to our own times to see them in true perspective. Of this much, however, we may feel certain; that the view that present conditions give rise for alarm will hardly command the assent of the thoughtful majority. Indeed, these very conditions may perhaps be a sign of better times to come, of new hope for the future.

Is it not that we have suddenly become sensitive to problems of social ethics rather than that such problems are assuming darker aspects than in the past thirty or forty years? The exposure of the Tweed ring in New York City indicated political corruption more shameless than any existing to-day, but it was followed by no such demands for sweeping reform as modern revelations of a less flagrant sort have called forth. We have really been meeting difficulties akin to those of the present day for many years, and the fact that we are now unusually conscious of these difficulties may not mean that they are more serious to-day than they were at times when the conscience of the country was comfortably at rest. It is characteristic of the English-speaking people to be jealous of their rights and privileges, and to stand out against oppression. It is characteristic of them, too, to preserve a sense of justice toward their fellows, and not to tolerate continued abuses of this justice. With a keen interest in practical affairs, they have always preserved an idealism of their own, which may sometimes seem to be slumbering, but which now and again breaks forth and manifests itself in unmistakable fashion. May it not be, then, that this finer side of our national character is now asserting itself, that all this restlessness of the present day is an outward and visible sign of the enduring power of civic ideals?

If we would truly understand the spirit of modern America, we must look across the water to Great Britain, the country which Hawthorne felicitously called "Our Old Home." Blood is still thicker than water, and we still share with our British cousins much the same political ideals, in spite of their sharper division into classes, and their monarchical form of government. Our kinship with them and our debt to them must not be lightly forgotten. The United States are often called a "melting-pot," into which are poured emigrants from many foreign nations, and out of which they emerge as the hardened metal of American citizens. Such foreigners have sometimes retained their national characteristics so strikingly that we think of so distinguished an American as Carl Schurz, who has often spoken in Cooper Union, as a German, of Petrosino as an Italian, or of Jacob Riis as a Dane, while we should all style the typically American Mr. Dooley "an Irishman." So we consider our democracy as the product of many such races rather than as the achievement of any one of them. This is true, but it ought not to make us forget that the beginnings of this national independence, which these men have done so much to strengthen, were due to English traditions and to English stock. In the words of Count Apponyi, we "combine audacity of progress with tenacity of tradition." We are fond of saying that the true spirit of modern America is the same which animated the men who wrote the Constitution. But the principles of the Revolutionary heroes were not the product of distinctively American conditions; they were fundamentally the same principles which had been brought over by the Pilgrims and the Puritans when they sailed to the New World. Contemporary European thought no doubt affected the phraseology of the Revolutionary watchwords, but even the germinating restlessness which culminated in the French Revolution was of secondary importance. The colonists had the courage to resist British oppression because they were of the same liberty-loving race as their adversaries, and it was because they were the direct inheritors of the spirit of Cromwell and Hampden that they had the vigor to make this resistance effective against overwhelming odds. The foundations of our republic rest on the sterling virtues of English character.

It is a curious fact that the foreigners who have done most to influence American democracy in the last hundred years have been, to a great extent, men of those very peoples which went to make up the parent English stock in the beginning. No one needs to be told that the English are a composite of Germanic and Scandinavian and French and Celtic elements, and that when Columbus discovered America these elements had only just been fused in the melting-pot of Britain, but we do not always remember that the Germans and the Scandinavians and the French and the Celts who come over to America nowadays add no really foreign elements to our blood, but strengthen it by the addition of the very elements of which it is partly composed already. They are mixed in the melting-pot of America, just as their forefathers were in the melting-pot of the British Isles. And they bring similar characteristics with them, — the persistence of racial distinctions is most surprising. The solidity of the Scandinavian, the enterprise of the German, the gayety of the French, the enthusiasm of the Celt, were the same a dozen centuries ago as they are to-day. These similarities must not, of course, be over-emphasized. National characteristics are now less easy to seize and to define; we are all such complex beings nowadays that it is difficult to distinguish these characteristics clearly. The bark is easily mistaken for the timber. But the contributions of foreign peoples to the American democracy of the nineteenth century are in many ways like the contributions of their ancestors to the making of the English stock many hundreds of years ago.

In the lectures to follow I propose that we look closely at these different races in the beginning, at the time when they were first combining to form the English people, that we observe their characteristics, and compare them with their descendants, who are now coming over to America and merging with a nation which was really made up of their own ancestors in the beginning. The very unlikeness of these races perhaps explains why the English-speaking group descended from them shows such a strange mixture of strength and weakness, and is less easily classified than are most European peoples. At the same time we may observe their early social progress, their advance from a simple and primitive community to a social system ruled by caste and governed for the sole interest of the upper classes, and finally to the beginnings of modern democracy, — the recognition of the rights of the people, and the demand on the part of the people themselves that their rights be considered.

There is, I believe, no better way for our purposes in which to do this than to review the great stories which sprang up among these different races in their formative period, stories which were handed down from generation to generation until the recital of them and the perpetuation of them became an inseparable part of national life. These old tales are interesting in themselves, they have triumphantly survived the test of time, they charm us to-day if we surrender ourselves to their spell, and they will charm our descendants after us. But more than this, such narratives are records of the thoughts and feelings of bygone peoples, they set forth the ideals for which those peoples strove, the vices they hated, the ambitions by which they were animated, more faithfully than historical documents can do. The stories themselves may be simple enough, but the details of the adventures, and the way in which the whole is told, show clearly what sort of a people has created an Arthur or a Roland or a Beowulf or a Reynard the Fox. Unconsciously, too, they voice the aristocratic or the democratic spirit as soon as class distinctions begin to prevail in these early communities. Through them we can follow the progress of the peoples who have made the English-speaking race, Saxon and Norman and Dane and Celt. In the limited time at our command we cannot, of course, undertake the difficult and complicated task of tracing the social history of the English people. What we are rather to do is to get a series of impressions, as vividly as may be, of certain significant periods, in which the very age and body of the time is, through these old tales, shown its own form and pressure.

First of all, we may look at the characteristics of that Germanic people, who, settling in Britain in the fifth century, laid the foundations of England as a nation.

In their great heroic poem 'Beowulf' appear those conceptions of honor, bravery, and self-sacrifice which still
mark what we call the Anglo-Saxon temperament.
Next, in the story of Roland and the knights of Charlemagne, the distinctive contribution of the French to
the development of English character will appear.   In
many ways the conquering Normans cherished higher
ideals than those whom they subdued, and the old
tradition that they marched into battle at Senlac to the
sound of the 'Song of Roland' may typify fitly enough
the victory of a folk whose hero was distinguished as
much for patriotism and piety as for prowess.   Still
another great advance is marked by the legends of
Arthur and the knights of the Round Table.   These
reveal a complete break with the institutions of earlier
times, a complete readjustment of social conventions,
not always for the better, but nevertheless making clear
to us why the word "chivalry" still stands to-day for
whatever is gentle and generous in the relations of men
and women.   They illustrate in great measure, too,
the characteristics of the Celtic temperament, — the
magic and mystery, the soaring imagination and "revolt
against the tyranny of fact" which marks such modern
work as the poetry of Mr. Yeats, with all its overlaid
modern romanticism.   The romances which relate the
quest of Arthur's knights for the Holy Grail form
particularly striking illustrations of the religious exaltation of the Middle Ages in its various manifestations.
No branch of the story of King Arthur has exercised
greater fascination upon men in all times than the legends
of the Grail.   But at this point we must observe another
side of the picture.   Despite their high ideals of courtesy

toward all men, the Arthurian romances are thoroughly aristocratic; the democratic spirit of the commons manifests itself in the ' History of Reynard the Fox,' that picturesque villain dear to the hearts of the Middle Ages, and in the story of Robin Hood, as told in the old English ballads. Both these worthies were loved for the enemies they made among the aristocracy; but while the rascally Reynard ignored law and defied justice, Robin Hood attempted to set things straight after his own fashion, by taking justice into his own hands. Reynard belongs rather to the imagination of the Continental peoples; but Robin Hood is a distinctively English creation, and in no way more so than that his actions reflect the English love of fair play, that they are not a glorification of clever and unscrupulous villainy. Finally, in the ' Canterbury Tales ' of Chaucer, we shall see all classes meeting on common ground for the first time since the Norman Conquest, their friendly relationship typifying the better social consciousness which ushers in modern history, the recognition of the rights of the people by the ruling aristocracy, the beginning of a democratic spirit for the English life of later times.

This will give merely a series of suggestions of the social ideals of certain significant periods; in the time at our disposal we cannot hope to carry the discussion farther than this. Our study will take no account of the thousand subtle and conflicting influences which so complicate the social history of any nation. It will call for no elaborate background of historical fact. There are the stories; it is for us to gather the meaning which lies beneath the surface, to see how it is that they are really the expression of national character. Their message is not less important because it has to be inferred. Historical documents state facts; whenever these stories present historic events, they distort them. What can be expected of a narrative which asserts that Charlemagne was two hundred years old, or which makes Arthur, originally a half-savage Celt skulking among the Welsh mountains, the peerless monarch of medieval chivalry? But it is the very deviations from history that are significant in these tales; not the events themselves, as historic facts. When the French make a new story out of the deeds of a Roland or an Arthur their very additions and alterations show what sort of a hero they considered most admirable, what qualities they cherished in a great national figure. All this is what gives life to history, if you admit that history should be the record of aspiration as well as of achievement.

You will observe that we are to deal wholly with early stories, not taking into account those of later times. The main reason for this limitation, as I have already said, is that we are concerned with the English people in the days when they were being welded into a nation, not with their subsequent development. But there is another reason, too. Modern literature is a far less trustworthy guide to the real sentiments of a people than is that of early times because it is full of the personal opinions and emotions of individual writers. When we read a modern novel, we are likely to think of the author as well as of the story. If we take up 'David Copperfield,' we are conscious of the presence of Dickens, and from every page of 'Vanity Fair' speaks the voice of Thackeray. Early story-telling, on the other hand, shows little of all this. The teller of the tale was of little account, the telling was the important thing. The relation between narrator and audience was completely different from the modern relation between novelist and reader. In order to understand this difference, we must think of a social and intellectual life very unlike our own.

In such a society as that of the Germanic tribes who invaded Britain and displaced the Celtic inhabitants of the island, a society which was in effect democratic, though organized on an aristocratic basis, all men, save the slaves, had a common share in traditions and privileges. A story was thus a part of the heritage of every man. He knew it well, and even if he could not repeat it as effectively as more gifted members of his tribe, he could tell it to his children, and they to their little ones in turn in the years to come. When stories were thus handed down by word of mouth, and when they might be told by anyone, every man was in a sense an author, since, if he chose, he might contribute his share toward the shaping of such a tale. He must not alter it too much, although he could hardly help introducing some slight variations of his own. But these variations must be such as to be accepted by his hearers, and even when the poet by profession gave a tale the final touches and the better-rounded form in which it may have ultimately been written down, there was nothing in his work which might not be understood and welcomed by everybody. This was the condition of affairs which brought 'Beowulf' into being, the 'Song of Roland' also, and in a far earlier time the Homeric poems. Such poetry represents, despite certain modernizations, the collective taste of the people as a whole, in a society thoroughly democratic in spirit. The poet himself, it will be observed, though he may have been admired as having a good voice and delivery, was not the inventor of the incidents, and he did not get his renown for treating such incidents in an individual or novel way. Men knew the tale, and wished it told as they knew it. They did not care about the poet's feelings; what they desired was the story itself.

After the feudal system was well established in Europe, when men felt themselves separated into more distinctly marked divisions, poets came to speak rather for a particular class than for the people as a whole. The century of the Norman Conquest marks a great change in this respect, not only in England, but all over Western Europe. The same story might please the lord in the hall, or his dependents, but it soon took on a different coloring as it was meant to appeal to the one class or the other. If the incidents were alike, the manner of telling them was different. But the poet, even when addressing the aristocracy, was frequently but little more concerned to emphasize his own thoughts and feelings than his brother of some centuries back had been, — he was anxious only that men should think that he was telling his tale aright, as it had been handed down by the earlier masters of his craft. Generally speaking, he cared little to have his name remembered. What he was especially likely to emphasize was his source, as a proof of the veracity of his statements — however colored by imagination these might be. Sometimes he referred to historical documents as his authority. Thus one Old French poem, 'The Song of the Saxons,' begins,

Whoever has the time and the desire to listen to my words and to remember them, let him be quiet, and he will learn a brave and noble song, *for which books of history are witness and guarantee.*

This medieval tradition of anonymity was not, of course, universal. Various authors might be cited who were desirous of securing personal approbation through the individuality of their tales, and whose chief interest lay in reshaping the story rather than in retelling it as they found it. We feel in the strongest way the personality of such men as Dante, Boccaccio, Chrétien de Troyes, Wolfram von Eschenbach. And Marie de France, the gifted lady who has left us such charming versions of the Breton lays, has told us her name, in order that, as she quaintly says, "it may be remembered." But these are the exceptions which prove the rule; the rank and file of the makers of medieval narrative aimed to be thought the mouthpieces of tradition. It must be borne in mind that we are here discussing only story-telling, and that such a type as the lyric, which by its very nature is subjective, lies outside our province.

Naturally, as we approach modern times, the author becomes more important, and as artistry of a conscious sort develops, the individual note becomes increasingly prominent. The poet begins to desire recognition for his work as well as for his skill as a performer; he wishes to have men observe his inventiveness or his character-drawing or the advance which he has made in some other way over known masters of authority. But not until the end of the Middle Ages, close to the time of the invention of printing, did the majority of writers have the courage to avow this, or did their work become rather the expression of their own personality than of the feelings of the audience for which they were working. This is true of only one of the poets here considered, the author of the 'Canterbury Tales,' who even appears in his own person, and, though he lets his characters speak for themselves, tells us plainly enough what he thinks about them. But even Chaucer depended often upon a show of sources as authorities, without troubling himself unduly about accuracy. Indeed, he seems on occasion to have put his tongue in his cheek, and slyly set down some sources which never existed!

How different the general attitude of the modern story-teller! Individuality, the creation of something distinctive and original, — this is his chief aim. He writes to impress his own convictions or feelings upon his audience, not to reflect for them their own. He is the last man to tell you he is imitating some one who has gone before him, or to assure you that he is telling things as he found them set down. Unless he can make such things different, he does not care to write of them, and it is most evident that he wishes you to perceive these excellent differences. So it comes about that much modern narrative poetry is written chiefly to give the poet a chance to reveal himself, or to bring a personal message, or to point a moral, or to dress up an old tale in such a way that it seems new because of its setting or its treatment. Think of Tennyson and the 'Idylls of the King,' with their Victorian morality so strangely plastered over them, of Byron's long poems, which display his own figure on every page, of Wordsworth's narrative verse, saturated with "my granddaddy's" philosophy, or of Swinburne's work, in which the story is almost hidden under superb and sensuous imagery. Scott had far more the medieval attitude than any of these men, for his long narrative poems make their effect primarily as good stories, simply and directly told, with little of the personal element intruding.

Thus the reflection of any great social movement is far more impersonal in medieval than in modern literature. It may be equally vivid in each, but the issue in modern times is likely to be deeply colored by the poet's own personal convictions and prejudices. An illustration will make this still clearer. The Crusades stirred Europe to the depths, but the reflection of this religious exaltation in narrative poetry was far more a reflection of the times in general than of the feelings of individuals. On the other hand, the influence of the French Revolution upon contemporary imaginative literature merely indicates how that great struggle reacted upon men of different temperaments. Consider the English poets, for example. Wordsworth and Byron and Shelley and Coleridge were all profoundly affected by the Revolution, but they uttered rather their own convictions than those of the English people as a whole. Though they may have thought themselves voicing the spirit of the times, they were really quite as much proclaiming their own views. No one of them was as impersonal in his utterances as was his brother of centuries before.

It sometimes happens that a modern poet succeeds completely in expressing the feelings of a great majority of the people on some social question, and utters these sentiments not so much for himself alone as for all his countrymen. His work thus becomes truly universal.　Perhaps the one man who has come nearest to striking the note of national idealism to-day is Rudyard Kipling.　He has for years been the real laureate of the British Empire, and his poetry has appealed to almost every class of readers in the United States.　He is "popular" in the best sense, because his verse strikes a responsive chord in all hearts.　His 'Recessional' owed its extraordinary vogue, not so much to its majestic rhythm and to its verbal felicity, as to the universal feeling it expressed, the same feeling which prompts reform in the United States to-day, — the danger of losing our souls in the quest for material things.　It made a most profound appeal to that public conscience which we have agreed is characteristic of the English-speaking people.

> God of our fathers, known of old,
>   Lord of our far-flung battle line,
> Beneath whose awful Hand we hold
>   Dominion over palm and pine —
> Lord God of Hosts, be with us yet,
> Lest we forget — lest we forget!
>
> The tumult and the shouting dies;
>   The captains and the kings depart:
> Still stands Thine ancient sacrifice,
>   An humble and a contrite heart.
> Lord God of Hosts, be with us yet,
> Lest we forget — lest we forget!
>
> Far-called, our navies melt away;
>   On dune and headland sinks the fire:
> Lo, all our pomp of yesterday
>   Is one with Nineveh and Tyre!
> Judge of the Nations, spare us yet,
> Lest we forget — lest we forget!

In this lyric, with its complete freedom from the personal note, and its expression of a universal sentiment, Kipling comes very close to the manner of medieval literature.   But he can be, in the next breath, intensely subjective, even while professing to phrase in verse the characteristic qualities of a great people.   In one of his less-known poems, 'An American,' he essays to describe our national type.

> Calm-eyed he scoffs at sword and crown,
>   Or panic-blinded, stabs and slays :
> Blatant he bids the world bow down,
>   Or cringing begs a crust of praise ;
>
> Or, somber-drunk, at mine and mart,
>   He dubs his dreary brethren Kings.
> His hands are black with blood: his heart'
>   Leaps, as a babe's, at little things.
>
>   *   *   *   *   *   *
>
> Enslaved, illogical, elate,
>   He greets th' embarrassed Gods, nor fears
> To shake the iron hand of Fate
>   Or match with Destiny for beers.

We all know that this is unfair, and that there is more than half a chance that Kipling would himself now acknowledge it to be so.   It is almost a pity to quote it ; the lapses of poets are generally better passed over in silence.   But it illustrates well enough the intrusion of the personal element into the work òf a poet who can, on occasion, speak for a whole race.

In these days of much scribbling, when we are so overwhelmed with books on every side, it is difficult to put ourselves into the right frame of mind to appreciate stories which did not spring from the desire of some author to be famous, or to make money, or to air his own convictions about life and art, but which arose from the hearts of the people themselves, which were told because they were interesting, and because by their example brave men and their children might be inspired to noble deeds. A "bold sincerity," to quote a phrase from Edmund Gosse, is the striking thing about all of them, — a novel quality for a public accustomed to the "six best sellers"! It is hard for us nowadays to escape from the tyranny of print; we are far indeed from the time when men got their tales by listening to them instead of reading them "printed an' bound in little books." To appreciate these properly, we must divest ourselves, so far as possible, of modern sophistication. Men of the Middle Ages were, in a sense, grown-up children, fond of a good story, not caring whence it came provided it were vouched for as an approved success, believing it religiously, with all its dragons and fairies, and resenting, just as children do to-day, any radical changes. Modern children are, indeed, the direct inheritors of these old tales. Many a boy can tell about Robin Hood as well as about Robinson Crusoe, and in his fairy-books he makes the acquaintance of old heroic stories of the past in lowlier estate. The legend of Brunhild and Sigurd or Siegfried, made familiar by Wagner in his 'Ring of the Nibelungen' music-dramas, is really the same story as 'The Sleeping Beauty in the Wood,' only with such differences as that in the fairy-tale the prince penetrates a hedge of sharp thorns instead of a wall of fire, and makes his way into a castle, instead of scaling a rocky height. If we would really understand these old tales,

then, we must bring to them something of the simplicity in the heart of a child. Otherwise the magic
will lose its potency, the valor of the knights will not
stir our pulses, the beautiful maidens will seem lay-
figures, and the giants and dragons clumsy inventions.

It is not the marvels, however, but the human quality of these tales which I would emphasize, the many
touches of nature which make that world akin to ours.
"Humanity," says Réné Doumic, "is ever the same.
Society is ever different." This is the whole point of
the lectures to follow, — to see how the aspirations
common to people in all ages manifested themselves
among our own ancestors ten centuries and more ago,
to see how much valor and love and patriotism and
ambition and avarice meant to them, and what they
thought about their own social relations to their fellow-
men. A study of these old stories is no antiquarian
pastime, no rummaging among dust, no quest for stiff
and soulless figures. It is the opening of the door upon
a life as exuberant as our own, full of richness and color,
stirred by adventure and by passion, with the sun shining bright in the heavens, and the joy of life strong in
the hearts of men. The phrase "medieval" sometimes
carries with it certain false notions, due largely to the
ignorance of our grandfathers, who knew little about
the period intervening between ancient and modern
times, and brushed it aside as unworthy of attention,
seeing in it only the ruin of the serener civilization of
classical antiquity and the supremacy of a ruder people
in Europe. They did not realize that this ruder people
were far more virile, and that they developed, in the
ten centuries from the fall of the Roman Empire to

the Discovery of America, a more vigorous civilization than the one they had supplanted.   They did not realize, either, that in this period, which we call the Middle Ages, are to be sought, to a large extent, the foundations of the great social and political institutions of modern times, that so far from being an era of universal decay, it was then that the seeds of a new spring were germinating, which have since burst into the full flower of a glorious summer.   So these tales of long ago will, if we take them aright, bring a message to our own times from the age which produced them. The idealism which we may believe we see manifesting itself in our national life to-day may be only a modern version of the idealism of our ancestors, as they have recorded it for us in the words and deeds of their great heroes.   The achievements of our present-day democracy may be only a reapplication to modern times of the best social impulses of the English-speaking people, in the days when they were still in the process of fusion into a single nation.

II

BEOWULF

The man who slew the dragon-brood
   A thousand years ago,
Is brother still to him who will
   Prevail against his foe.

The Saxon blood still warms at flood
   The veins of living men,
And Celt and Gaul are still at call
   To give the strength of ten.

A thousand leagues across the seas
   There comes their far-sent cry,
"We gave you life, in sweat and strife;
   Be men, ere yet ye die!"

II

BEOWULF

THE English-speaking peoples have always taken
particular pride in being considered intensely patriotic.
Both British and Americans have manifested, even in
the midst of grave national crises, a sturdy loyalty to
their own country, a determination to stand by it
through thick and thin, to silence its detractors, and to
punish its enemies. They have indeed often carried
their enthusiasm too far. In proclaiming the superiority
of their native land over all others on the globe, they
have now and again irritated their neighbors, so that
the jingoism of John Bull and the self-sufficiency of
Uncle Sam have become proverbial. This is no new
development of English character during the past few
centuries; English literature is full of patriotic pride
in the great events of national history, and of visions
of glories to come in the future. Shakspere, to cite
only one magnificent example, well illustrates both the
devotion and the bluster of the English temper. His
play of 'Henry the Fifth' is a full-throated glorification
of English valor and virtue, — the spirit of Agincourt
quickened by the political successes of the reign of
Queen Elizabeth. But he is unfair to the French;
they were brave warriors, yet he represents them as

cowards; they had much justice on their side, but he sets forth the English cause as altogether right and holy. The whole play is designed to exhibit the greatness of England, — a "little body with a mighty heart." This intensity of patriotism, which concedes nothing to others and arrogates everything to itself, is, it must be acknowledged, fairly typical of English character.

It is very surprising, then, in turning to the oldest English epic, to find that there is nothing patriotic about it at all. We call it an English poem, and rightly. It was written on English soil, for Englishmen, and in the English tongue. It was known in various parts of the country, as is shown by the traces of different dialects in which it was successively told. In temper and spirit it is thoroughly in accord with all we can learn about our Anglo-Saxon ancestors during the two or three centuries following their invasion of Britain. We know, too, that it had been in their possession for some time before it assumed its present shape; that it was not a mere translation from another tongue. Yet the epic deals neither with English people nor with English heroes. Some of the tribes which had settled in Britain are mentioned, but in an altogether unimportant way. The peoples whom it celebrates are foreigners, Scandinavians. The home of the hero is apparently in the Scandinavian peninsula, although we cannot be sure, and the scene of the poem is laid partly in that land of gloomy waters and long, dark winters, and partly in Denmark. The Danish people are very prominent; the poem opens with a glorification of their power, and loses no opportunity to sing their praises. This race was in later times actively hostile to the English; we all remember how the Vikings, those savage sea-robbers, swept down on the coast of Britain, pillaging and burning, until they were finally strong enough to seize the very government of the country, and to place a Danish king on the English throne. It was resistance to these Scandinavian invaders which developed much of the national spirit that arose in the reign of King Alfred, yet even then this epic, which exalted England's enemies, continued to be popular. The unique manuscript in which the poem is preserved dates from the tenth century, when struggles between the Danes and the Anglo-Saxons were constant and bitter. In short, ' Beowulf ' is a story dealing with foreign subject-matter, borrowed from an alien and even hostile people, with no trace of English patriotism about it. How is this strange situation to be explained ?

The answer is simple. At the time when 'Beowulf' was composed in the form in which we now have it, the English were unable to produce any truly national literature because they had as yet developed no political solidarity. They had not yet come to think of themselves as a single people, united by common interests and ideals; they were still in an unsettled condition, governed by various petty kings, and continually warring against each other. They were all so much occupied by these internal contests that they had little opportunity to feel the ties of blood or of governmental organization. These conditions are reflected in their poetry; patriotic literature can hardly develop in a constantly divided state. True national unity was rare in Europe in those days; the English were not

e in this respect. The Continent was still most
ttled, — the various peoples were wandering rest-
lessly about, constantly forsaking their old homes and
seeking new habitations. Even when stationary for a
time, they led a troubled existence, in which defense of
their own possessions was varied chiefly by efforts to
seize the possessions of others. Fighting was the main
business of life, the conquest of treasure and territory
its goal, and a settled and peaceful existence almost
unknown. The whole era in which this epic grew up
is fitly called the Migration Period. Some few peoples,
as for example the Danes, were able to develop further
toward what we should call a national consciousness,
but they were more fortunate than most of their neighbors. Out of all this confusion there came, in the fullness of time, the beginnings of the orderly governments
of modern Europe. The process was slow, however,
and for the evolution of great heroic tales like 'Beowulf' we have to think of an age when the sentiment
of the people was tribal rather than national, heroic
rather than patriotic.

The achievements of a warrior of that day were likely
not to be closely associated with his native country.
The typical champion was a wanderer on the face of
the earth, going wherever glory called him. He was,
of course, devoted to his lord and to his comrades, and
bound to defend them and the hearths and homes of
his people whenever occasion arose. But if he gained
merely personal renown, if he uttered mighty boasts
over the evening ale-cups, and afterwards performed
heroic actions, he was accounted quite as admirable
as if he helped to sustain the integrity of a larger politi-

cal organization. It was a common thing for a warrior to seek service under a foreign prince, leaving his
own folk to fight their battles alone. In a time of con-
tinual warfare, such additions to the military efficiency
of a tribe were sure to be welcome, and any stranger of
proved bravery was given a cordial reception. There
must have been a certain fascination, too, in those days
of restricted horizons, about a man who had journeyed
from afar, especially if he were crowned with the glory
of successful achievement. And foreign heroes who
came in song and story were as warmly welcomed as
those who came in the flesh. It is hardly too much to
say that the most popular figures of heroic story were
those adopted from foreign peoples. The Scandinavians celebrated Sigurd or Siegfried, for example,
though he was a German hero, closely associated with
the river Rhine. From these Scandinavian sources
Richard Wagner took, in the main, the material for
his great 'Rheingold' tetralogy, because he found them
more deeply poetic than the German versions. Both
Scandinavians and Germans in the old days sang of
the exploits of Dietrich of Bern, who was Theodoric,
king of the Goths. People were generally more interested in a hero fighting for his own glory than in a
hero battling for his own country. They wanted to
hear of his deeds; it did not greatly matter whether
these were patriotic or not.

It is worth noting that the popularity of heroes from
foreign lands continued even into the time when a truly
national spirit had developed among the peoples of
Western Europe. If a champion had gained great
renown among his own people through patriotic defense

of his country against its enemies, his brilliant exploits
were sufficient to insure his fame, not only at home, but
abroad as well. We shall see, in a later lecture, how the
valor of Roland, who died for France in the passes of
the Pyrenees, was celebrated all over Europe. And the
French people themselves, despite these native traditions, were greatly interested in heroes from other
peoples. Along with such stories as those centering
about Charlemagne and his knights, they adopted those
of the British hero Arthur, raising him to an eminence
which he had never gained among men of his own race,
and finally making him a more splendid and imposing
figure than Charlemagne himself.

All this explains why it was easy for the Anglo-Saxons
to adopt the foreign hero Beowulf. The main theme
of the story, it will be noted, is the valor of one man, a
man fighting, in the main, not for his country, but for
his own renown. There is much high-sounding praise
of the Danes and of the Geats, but the real interest
centers in neither people, but in the champion who engages in desperate fights against demons and dragons.
The note which is struck at the beginning of the poem

Lo, we have heard of the glory of the Spear-Danes!

must not mislead us, for it becomes evident when we
turn to the story itself that this enthusiasm for the
Danish people is only incidental. The Danes are ruled
by a great king named Hrothgar, successful in war and
wise in peace. As a symbol of his power and glory he
builds a great hall in which his warriors may feast
through the long winter nights, and in which he himself
may sit in state, presiding over their revels, and dispens-

ing treasure. But a great misfortune befalls him and
his people. A demon called Grendel, half demon, half
like a gigantic bear in shape, angered at the revelry
in the hall, comes creeping from his lair in a haunted
pool in the forest, stealthily advancing through the
low-hanging mists of the evening, and attacks the warriors as they lie asleep after their feasting. Night
after night he comes, until no one dares sleep in the
hall, and "the best of buildings" stands empty and
useless. He devours his victims, crushing their bones
and drinking their blood. Often some Danish warrior
plans vengeance, vowing over the wine-cups that he will
abide the coming of the demon in the hall, and slay
him. But when morning breaks, the benches are all be-
spattered with blood, and the daring warrior is missing.
Twelve long winters this continues; the pride of the
great king is turned into sorrow, and his counselors
can devise no means of redress from the foe. Then
Beowulf, a stranger from the land of the Geats, in the
north, comes to the aid of the suffering Danish people,
meets the monster in the haunted hall, wounds him to
the death by tearing off his arm, and afterwards pursues his ogress-mother, who comes to avenge her son,
into the depths of her lair in the fens, and kills her.

In spite of all the glowing rhetoric about the glory
of the Spear-Danes, then, they have to be helped out of
a tight place because they have no champion valiant
enough at home. Surely this is not the best of ways
to exalt them! As a matter of fact, the poet, in such a
line as that just quoted, merely desires to assure his
hearers that they are to be told of the fortunes of a
noble race. The people of Beowulf are duly celebrated,

which enhances his glory as their king, but the poem is no expression of the patriotism of the Geats. Such poetry as this disdains characters who are not exalted; it gains double impressiveness by narrating the experiences of mighty peoples. It deals with the heroic deeds of heroic men, — who these men are does not greatly matter, but they should not come of inferior stock. The poet is interested in contemporary history, but with as impartial a point of view as a New York newspaper discussing European politics. The various nations which are mentioned from time to time are never belittled; the spirit of the whole poem is much like that of the Iliad, in which enthusiasm for the Greeks does not prevent an equal sympathy for the Trojans. The heroic epic is almost always sportsmanlike; it delights in a fair fight between well-matched adversaries, and recognizes that the more valiant the adversary, the greater is the glory of the hero.

The epic of 'Beowulf' really consists of two elements; first, old tales about champions who killed supernatural creatures hostile to mankind, and second, Germanic history and legend, which serves as a background. In the course of time, fairy-tales and history have become so fused as to appear like one; the old stories have been applied to a Germanic hero and placed in a realistic setting. Men in Scandinavian lands on the Continent sang of the exploits of this hero in short lays, or epic songs, which were later brought to England by minstrels, and there molded into epic form. The present shape of the poem is probably due largely to one man, about two hundred years before the death of King Alfred. Grateful as we must be for his work, we must

not forget that he is only in a small degree the author.
The real name of the author, as Gilbert Murray says
of the Greek epic, is Legion, — the many men who
sang of these deeds before there was any developed
epic at all. In some such way as this we may conceive
the present poem to have taken shape. Let us now
look more closely at each of the two main elements,
fairy-tale and history, which have gone to the making
of the whole.

The three great contests with supernatural beings,
— Grendel, his mother, and the fiery dragon, — en-
gage the chief interest in the poem; everything else
is merely secondary. And what good stories they are!
How impressive is the picture of Beowulf, keeping
watch alone in the haunted hall, waiting for the coming
of the monster Grendel, who presently approaches,
plucks open the door of the hall, and glares ferociously
into the darkness within! Out of his eyes starts a
loathsome light, like a lambent flame. Quickly he
seizes one of the sleeping warriors, and tears him to
pieces, swallowing him alive in great mouthfuls, and
exulting in his horrid feast. But on a sudden Beowulf
stands up, and grapples with him. No weapon is used;
the prodigious strength of the hero is pitted against
the supernatural power of the demon. Fiercely they
struggle, the great hall reëchoes, the benches are over-
turned, — it is a contest such as men have never seen.
At last Grendel realizes that he has met his match, and
strives to escape, but not until Beowulf has torn off
his arm at the shoulder is he able to flee to his lair,
wounded unto death. As morning breaks there is great
rejoicing, the hall is magnificently adorned, and a great

feast is held.   Rich gifts are bestowed on the hero,
and many men come to look at the gigantic arm and
shoulder of the demon, which are hung up as a trophy.
But all rejoicing is turned into grief on the ensuing
night, when the mother of Grendel, a ferocious she-
demon, and only less terrible than her son as a woman
is less powerful than a man, breaks into the hall, and
in the absence of the hero, carries off a valiant Danish
warrior to her haunt in the forest lake.   Beowulf
straightway resolves to search out this abode, which
King Hrothgar describes in graphic words : —

They dwell in a region unvisited by men, wolf-cliffs and windy
headlands and dangerous pathways through the fens, where the
water-fall [1] descendeth, shrouded in the mists of the heights, a flood
under the overhanging rocks.   It is not far hence in measure of miles
that the mere lieth.   Over it hang trees covered with hoar-frost, with
roots firm fixed they overshadow the waters.   There at night may a
ghostly wonder be seen, — a fire on the flood !   So wise is none of the
children of men as to know what lieth in those depths.   Although
the heath-rover, the stag with mighty horns, may seek out this
grove, driven thither from afar, he will sooner yield up his life upon
the bank than plunge in and hide his head beneath the waters.   Uncanny is the place.   There the weltering of waters mounteth up,
pale unto the heavens, when the wind waketh evil weathers, until
the air darkles and the heavens weep.

Nothing daunted, Beowulf journeys to the haunted
mere, dives into its depths, slays the ogress, cuts off
the head of the dead Grendel, as a trophy, or to keep
his spirit from troubling men, and returns in triumph

[1] I have ventured to introduce a rendering of my own for the lines
describing the mountain stream.   This translation seems to me
at once more picturesque and more plausible than the usual interpretation, and fully in accord with Anglo-Saxon idiom.

to the hall, now forever delivered from its terrors. Richly laden with gifts, he sails back again to his own country in the north, where he ultimately becomes king, rules gloriously for fifty years, and dies in slaying a dragon which has attacked his people.

These adventures of Beowulf at the Danish court are, it will be observed, pure fantasy, arising not from the stern realities of a nation's existence, but from universal popular imagination. It is all indeed a fairy-tale, which happens to have been localized in a definite country and given a historical background, but is none the less essentially imaginary. This particular story of a man who slays demons which menace a hall or house is very widespread. Men of many different countries have told it with bated breath, when the raging weather of a tempestuous winter made all nature seem alive with uncanny monsters unfriendly to mankind. In spite of the changes which such a story suffers in many tellings, we can trace it all over Europe, and even in other continents. There is no particular reason, apparently, why it should have been localized in Denmark; every country was in early times troubled by such spooks as Grendel and his dam. Nowadays we never see them; they have all been killed off by the valor of heroes and by the skepticism of an unbelieving age. But they were very real and dangerous in the good old times, — the natural foes to everything joyous and winsome, and their ugly natures were stirred to the depths by the revelry of heroes in the night-time. The poet reflects, with a touch of compassion, that they got no pleasure out of life. These joyless incarnations of evil are a most interesting manifestation of the popular

imagination. They have little foundation in reality;
they are merely phantoms of the brain, like the monsters of classical times, — the Minotaur slain by Theseus,
the Chimera destroyed by Bellerophon, or Medusa,
whose snaky head was severed from her body by Per-
seus. It is with such stories as these that 'Beowulf'
belongs, — a very different type from such heroic adventures as that of Horatius at the bridge, or of Leoni-
das holding the pass at Thermopylæ. There the patriotic note is the controlling element, and the whole
is founded upon a historical fact or upon a legend accepted as true; here history has no place, save as a
means of making the story seem real.

The fight with the dragon, the third great adventure
of the poem, is another creation of fantasy. Dragons
were an even commoner affliction than monsters such
as Grendel. They were a strange but well-accepted
species in natural history, no more unfamiliar to people
in those days than the kangaroo or the hyena is to us.
It was their nature to seek out extorted treasure in
the womb of earth, and to guard it with their glittering
folds. From this they derived no particular pleasure;
it was instinct which drove them to do it. But the
real reason why most dragons existed seems to have
been to provide heroes with something to kill. Whenever a dragon appears in these old stories, a champion
can almost always be discerned on the horizon, on
his way to slay it. In our epic, the monster watches
over a priceless treasure in a rocky cavern, but he is
irritated by an unwelcome visitor, and revenges himself by laying waste the country with his fiery breath.
So the hero Beowulf, now grown old and gray, seeks

him out with a small band of followers. The dragon,
brooding over the treasure in his lair under a hoary
rock, hears the clear voice of the warrior bidding him
come forth, and in anger he writhes out of his cavern,
curving like a bow in sinuous folds, and spewing forth
fire and flame. The struggle between the dragon and
the old hero is terrible; the monster almost prevails,
but in Beowulf's hour of need a young warrior comes
to his assistance. After a frightful combat the veno-
mous serpent is slain, but not before Beowulf has received a severe wound. The poison proves too mighty
for the aged hero to resist, and so he dies, even in the
hour of victory. His body is burnt on a great funeral
pyre, with solemn ceremonial. The dead dragon is
flung from the top of the lofty cliff into the sea breaking on the rocks beneath.

The whole framework of the story is imaginary, then,
and even absurd. Such fairy-tale incidents as these
seem indeed rather childish for the supporting structure
of a great heroic tale. But this is not at all the impression which the epic itself makes. No such thought
occurs to us when we read it. The setting in which the
whole is placed is so realistic, — the courts and domains
of the Scandinavian kings are so graphically described,
that even the killing of spooks and dragons seems
realistic too. The constant references to historical
and traditional events, represented as contemporary,
help still more to make the main action seem plausible.
Fiction may almost be elevated into the realm of fact
if it is mingled with veracious history. King Hrothgar,
who built the great hall, is a historical character, he
actually held his court in Denmark, as the poem states.

Of Hygelac, too, there are definite and trustworthy records in history. He lost his life in an unsuccessful expedition into the Low Countries in the early sixth century, against a combined army of Franks and Frisians. It is easier to believe a ghost story if the ghost appears in the house of a man whom we know, and when we remember that there is a certain amount of sober fact in this tale it becomes easier to accept Grendel. Moreover, this setting adds dignity to the action, it raises the whole tone of the story in such a way that whatever triviality there may be about it disappears. Among such surroundings as those of King Hrothgar's court, it is no longer a Jack the Giant-killer yarn. It is serious and tragic ; it has all the dignity of epic poetry.

Early literature is full of such achievements as this, full of the transformation of fairy-tales into narratives which seem true through the realism of their setting, the dignity of their treatment, and the individualization of their characters. In the lectures to follow we shall see abundant illustrations of this, but modern literature as well affords plenty of examples. Shakspere's tragedy of 'King Lear' is built up about an old popular tale of a king and his three daughters, which is still told to-day by the peasants of Europe, — a tale quite as trivial as the one which underlies the first two adventures of 'Beowulf.' But so wonderful is the delineation of character in 'King Lear' that we forget the essential absurdity of the plot. The same is true of the 'Merchant of Venice.' But Shakspere has placed the story of Portia and the caskets — another old tale — and the episode of the bond exacted by Shylock in

so veracious a background that the improbability of a
lady's choosing a husband by mere chance, or of a man's
forfeiting his life to lend money for his friend's wooing,
is entirely forgotten.   The stock of plots in literature,
medieval as well as modern, is limited ; the transformations of these plots in the hands of succeeding generations are endless.   Sometimes we do not recognize these
old motives when they are applied to scenes with which
we are ourselves familiar.   One of the most popular
plays produced in New York in recent years presented
in its opening scene the interior of a flat in Harlem,
but the plot was a modification of that used by Shakspere in 'Measure for Measure.'   As a plot, it was not
new in Shakspere's play ; he borrowed it from a contemporary drama, which in its turn was based upon a
short story in Italian.   The same situation has been
used by modern dramatists, now in a Japanese setting,
and again thrown against the vivid background of life
in Italy a hundred years ago.   So the men who took
this old tale about the slaying of monsters and gave it
to a Scandinavian hero were merely doing what has been
done in all ages, — they were bringing a good story
up to date.

The danger in such a proceeding as this is that the
story may not quite fit into its setting, that the hero
or the heroine may not act quite naturally in new surroundings.   So when this fairy-tale champion, the
slayer of dragons and monsters, is set down in the midst
of a very different society from that to which he has
been accustomed, he sometimes shows traces of his
earlier character.   He is made a king, but he is only
a king for the purposes of the story, because a hero as

great as he ought to have that dignity. He is hardly as real a monarch as the lesser rulers of neighboring states; the poem has little to say of the political events of his long reign of fifty years, while it is full of the events in other nations. Almost all the poem says about his reign is, "Then unto Beowulf did the broad kingdom fall, and well did he rule it for fifty winters. He was a wise king, the aged guardian of the land. And so time passed, until a dragon began to reveal his power in the darkness of the night,"—and with the dragon we get once more into the realm of fantasy. When he slays this monster, the poem represents his act, in the main, not as a piece of self-sacrifice, on behalf of his people, but as the crowning achievement of a heroic career, a defense of his title as the mightiest of warriors, which will bring him, if he wins, a substantial reward in the hoard of gold and jewels. In order to show his strength and valor, he attacks the monster single-handed. He would even like to fight him with bare hands, unaided by weapons, as he did Grendel, if it were feasible. He feels that no hero less valiant than himself ought to attempt to slay the dragon; he says to his warriors, "It is no adventure for you, nor is it meet for any man, save for me alone, to measure might with the monster and achieve glory in fighting him. By my prowess will I win the gold, or else battle, a perilous risking of life, shall take away your lord." He thinks more of his own renown than about the sufferings of his people, apparently, and in his dying hour he wishes the gold and jewels brought to him so that he may feast his eyes upon them, "and thus, having seen the store of treasure, the easier yield up life and the lordship

which I long have held." If such a comparison may
be ventured, it might be said that Beowulf engages in
the contest with the dragon in about the spirit of the
modern prize-fighter who faces a challenging opponent
in the ring, who is eager to win for the sake of winning,
but who thinks also of the purse which awaits the victor
at the end. Beowulf sometimes betrays his plebeian
origin, showing us that before he was made an illustrious
prince and a king in a stately epic, he was once a crude
demon-killing champion, desiring nothing more lofty
than to be rich and famous.

All this accords ill with the conception of Beowulf
as the ideal Germanic king, a conception clearly in the
mind of the poet of the epic. Indeed, Beowulf is himself conscious of his responsibilities. At the very end,
as his death draws near, he remembers with satisfaction
that he has done his duty as a sovereign. "Fifty years
have I ruled this people; yet never has there been a
king of all the neighboring tribes who has dared make
war against me, sought to terrify me. In my home
I awaited what time might bring me, held well mine
own, sought no treacherous feuds, swore no false oaths.
In all this can I rejoice, though sick unto death with
my wounds." And at his funeral, when the warriors,
the sons of athelings, rode about the burial mound
and lamented the death of their lord, they not only
"praised his heroism and fittingly commended his deeds
of valor," but they also said that he was "a mighty
king, the mildest and most gracious, the gentlest to
his people, and the most eager for praise." In aiming
to show that Beowulf was distinguished as a sovereign,
the epic often mentions his royal virtues, but it only

partially succeeds in suppressing the earlier conception
of his character as a hero of mere brute force.

We see, then, how necessary it is to observe the way
in which these great stories developed, if we are to judge
of them as reflections of social ideals. Such a poem
as this becomes doubly significant when we perceive
that it reveals two different stages in human culture;
while if we try to reconcile these conflicting conceptions,
we are led to nothing but confusion and error. As it
is, we can see that the ideals of earlier times would no
longer serve for those who gave the poem its present
shape, that men had come to demand in a hero something more than a mere display of physical strength,
although that may still be the controlling interest.
I can scarcely insist too strongly, then, that we must
study most carefully the origin and development of the
stories which we are to consider in the lectures to follow.
Only by such procedure is sound criticism possible.
How many men have been misled, in striving to pluck
out the heart of the mystery in the play of 'Hamlet,'
by failing to make allowances for the influence of the
crude old story of blood and revenge on which it is
based! When the reflective and scholarly Hamlet,
"the glass of fashion and the mold of form," startles
us by such words as "now could I drink hot blood,"
we get an echo of the earlier and cruder conception of
his character, just as when Beowulf appears to think
only of his own glory in performing a deed which is to
deliver his people from a terrible affliction.

It has even been thought that we may trace a still
earlier stage of development in the story, that the hero
was once not a mortal at all but a divinity, a god of

summer or of light, perhaps, whose victory over Grendel is merely a symbol of the conquest of winter or of darkness by the bright and beneficent forces of nature. It has also been suggested that Grendel may stand for the malarial mists of the Low Countries, which rack the bones of men with fever, just as Grendel crunched them in his teeth, and that the hero was once a wind-god who blew all such pestilential vapors far away. Such theories as these are misleading; there is no way of proving them, nor indeed, of disproving them. The vivid imagination of early peoples undoubtedly personifies the forces of nature, but that does not mean that every spook or dragon in early story is merely a symbol for some one of these forces. A giant was probably a giant to most men; a dragon was a dragon. There is no indication in this poem that the case was different. And so if we take the poem as it stands, and think of Beowulf as a mortal, and of his adversaries only as particularly ugly bugaboos, we shall not be leaning upon shaky interpretations to which the text gives no support.

It is part of Beowulf's glory that while his exploits are chiefly against supernatural creatures, he is himself only a human being. He is very strong; his strength, like Sir Galahad's, is as the strength of many men, not because his heart is pure, however, but because his biceps is hard. This is all, except his ability to exist under water, when he dives into the haunted pool to kill the ogress. This was a power often vouchsafed to mortals in early story; it is indeed familiar enough in modern tales of the supernatural. Matthew Arnold's touching little poem of the 'Forsaken Merman' tells of a mortal maiden who went to dwell under the waters,

but was so much a mortal that she was unhappy until
she could get back to earth once more. Beowulf has
no advantages but his strength and courage; by these
alone he wins. Had he at his command the magic which
protects Grendel, or the fiery defense of the dragon,
or the supernatural powers of a demigod, the credit for
his victories would be so much the less.

He is aided by no divinities from above, although he
piously gives the Lord thanks for his victory. The epic
is very different in this respect from the 'Iliad,' in which
the struggles of men are constantly decided by the gods,
who descend to earth in person, turn the tide of battle,
bicker over their favorites, and are altogether human
in their partiality. The final outcome of the struggles
about windy Troy is mainly due to their intervention,
not to the superior valor of certain of the contestants.
It hardly seems fair to the Homeric heroes to have their
best efforts go for naught by the operation of forces
over which they have no control. There is nothing of
all this in 'Beowulf.' If pagan deities ever played
an important part, they have vanished from the
story. The Christian Lord of Hosts is the God of
Battles, but though He directs the universe, He does
not interfere in the fighting. Beowulf knows the issue
is in the hands of the Lord, but depends on his own
strength. In the contest with the mother of Grendel
he makes a successful resistance, so the poet reminds us
piously, because the Lord is on his side, but mainly because his corselet is thick. He puts his trust in Heaven,
but he keeps his powder dry. The hand of God is
manifested in Beowulf's struggles in about the same way
that it was in the battle of Waterloo.

The poem is, of course, fundamentally pagan in spirit. It has acquired a veneer of Christianity, but this is in places so thin that the older material underneath may be clearly discerned. For this alteration the poet who put the story into the form in which we read it to-day was probably responsible. He tried to make it over into a good religious tale, introducing many references to the Lord, and making Grendel's black soul still blacker by deriving him from Cain, the progenitor of so many evil monsters. But the change was only partly successful. Although Beowulf has been transformed into a good devout Christian, with his mouth full of pious phrases, he is still a good deal of a heathen at heart. He forgets his new religion frequently, after the manner of other newly converted savages, sometimes attributing death and destruction to Wyrd, the heathen goddess, and neglecting God completely in his reflections as to the way in which the universe is ruled. Unfortunately, this new and incongruous material has been inlaid into the main substance of the story in such a way that it cannot be taken out without destroying the beauty of the whole. Portions of the original have undoubtedly been sacrificed to make room for it. It cannot be removed without leaving ugly holes and gaps; the whole effect, however incongruous, is better if it be allowed to stand.

One of the mourners at Beowulf's funeral pyre is his aged wife, who utters a mournful lament for the departed hero, and foresees evil days to come. Nothing at all has been said of her earlier in the poem; we are completely ignorant of her lineage and her character, and of the circumstances which led to her coming as

a bride to the court of the king of the Geats. Striking
indeed is the contrast to later poetry, in which the love-
affairs of the hero are often of equal interest with his
warlike exploits. In this epic as a whole, woman
occupies a decidedly minor place. Kings are appro-
priately provided with queens, who are properly deco-
rative, but who arouse little interest. Royal marriages
in the surrounding nations are often mentioned, but for
the sake of politics rather than of sentiment. There
is little suggestion of the love of youth and maiden,
of husband and wife. The affection of parents for
children is occasionally recalled; when Beowulf goes to
Denmark to slay the monster Grendel, the Danish queen,
in a pretty passage, attempts to enlist the sympathies
of the great foreign hero in the fortunes of her sons,
should they ever stand in need of assistance. But
love of any sort has little place in this poem; it is supplanted by the sterner emotions. The heroes care
much more for their proud names as warriors than they
do for love or life or religion. Hence the whole seems
a little cold and hard, a little lacking in human sympathy. It may arouse admiration; it seldom touches
the heart.

Moreover, this epic is in many ways aristocratic, with
something of the aristocrat's pride and coldness. It
was obviously intended for refined and educated circles,
not for ruder listeners or readers. These old popular
fairy-tale adventures have acquired a prodigious
amount of dignity in being transferred to the courts
of the Scandinavian kings. At these courts there is a
deal of elaborate etiquet, — no rude barbarian manners.
A foreign ambassador at Versailles in the time of

Louis XIV can hardly have been received with more ceremony than was Beowulf when he arrived at the palace of King Hrothgar, upon his landing in Denmark. The hero was not allowed to walk straight into the royal presence and state his errand; he and his warriors were obliged to wait outside until they had been summoned by the herald, and given permission to enter. This functionary did not abate one jot of the usual formalities; "he knew the custom of the court," and did not permit even so distinguished a stranger as Beowulf to enter the hall until he had first been announced. And Beowulf, on his part, went through all the formalities in the proper way, as a prince, one well versed in all matters of etiquet, ought to do. In all this ceremony the epic poet takes manifest pleasure. He has none of the free and easy attitude of the popular story-teller towards royal personages; he treats them with the greatest seriousness, even telling us, first and last, a great deal about the proper sort of conduct for kings and queens. Yet a king was in this society not much superior to the ruling warrior class which surrounded him, save by virtue of the rank which they had themselves conferred upon him. If the ruler of the Danes maintained the ceremony of a Louis XIV, he did not enjoy so much power. He could not have said "I am the State;" he was its head only by consent of those who would otherwise be his peers. He had very definite duties towards his followers, — he took the lead in war and in government, and he was obliged to dispense treasure liberally to those about him. Stinginess was universally condemned as one of the worst possible faults for a king to have. Social relations at this period are not wholly clear, but it is evident that the society, though aristocratic, was comparatively simple. There were few elaborate distinctions of rank, and service as a warrior was in itself a title to honor. With the slave and the freedman such poetry as this refuses to deal. It is not snobbish, but it does not hold the actions of meaner men to be fit themes for heroic song.

We may call the social body represented in 'Beowulf' a democratic aristocracy. It is ruled by the king and by the powerful nobles, but those who do not occupy exalted positions are not despised. There is a certain large simplicity about the intercourse of men with each other, as there is in the performance of their deeds of valor. The situation is much like that in the Old French 'Song of Roland,' which we are presently to consider. [This poem and 'Beowulf' have often been called heroic, in contradistinction to those of the epoch which followed, the era of feudalism and chivalry, the age of medieval romance. In the later or romantic period there is always a certain condescension in the relation of lord to commoner.] Distinctions of caste affect all the relationships of life; the man of gentler birth feels himself in every way the superior being. But Beowulf and his warriors, or Hrothgar and the men gathered in his hall, or Roland and the Twelve Peers of France, think far less about their exalted rank; they are content to assume the responsibilities of leadership, without affecting to ignore those for whom these duties have been undertaken. They are no less noble, but they are less haughtily conscious of their nobility.]

[The epic of 'Beowulf,' then, proclaims the glory of the most incomparable of heroes, placed in the highest

position in the ruling class of a warlike and democratic,
yet cultivated and highly conventionalized society. It
portrays the marvelous valor of such a champion, who
is obliged to contend against adversaries of super-
human powers, and it exalts before all things else his
courage and physical strength. Yet it conceives him
as a human being, with no relish of divinity about him,
no advantages not vouchsafed to mortals. It further
emphasizes the ideal virtues of the hero as king, —
generosity, ambition, moderation, wisdom. By implication and by precept it sets forth the beauty of
devoted service and the baseness of treachery. It is
the epic of the smaller state, of the tribe rather than of
the nation, hence it is lacking in patriotic fervor. It is
the epic of converted paganism, in which the heathen
belief is not wholly dead, and the Christianity not wholly
spontaneous, hence it is lacking in religious emotion.
It is the epic of brute force, hence it is lacking in the
softer feelings of mankind, in the love of wife and of
child. Perhaps it is not too much to assert, however,
that in its lofty spirit, its vigor, and its sincerity, it
truly represents the foundations of the modern Anglo-
Saxon character, that it reflects traits which unite British
and Americans at the present day, traits which are
distinctive of English-speaking people throughout the
world.

III

THE SONG OF ROLAND

J'aime le son du cor, le soir, au fond des bois,
Soit qu'il chante les pleurs de la biche aux abois,
Ou l'adieu du chasseur que l'écho faible accueille,
Et que le vent du nord porte de feuille en feuille.

Que de fois, seul, dans l'ombre à minuit demeuré,
J'ai souri de l'entendre, et plus souvent pleuré !
Car je croyais ouïr de ces bruits prophétiques
Qui précédaient la mort des Paladins antiques.

O montagne d'azur ! ô pays adoré !
Rocs de la Frazona, cirque de Marboré,
Cascades qui tombez des neiges entraînées,
Sources, gaves, ruisseaux, torrents des Pyrénées ;

Monts gelés et fleuris, trône des deux saisons,
Dont le front est de glace et le pied de gazons !
C'est là qu'il faut s'asseoir, c'est là qu'il faut entendre
Les airs lointains d'un cor mélancolique et tendre.

  * * * * * * *

Ames des Chevaliers, revenez-vous encor ?
Est-ce vous qui parlez avec la voix du cor ?
Roncevaux ! Roncevaux ! dans ta sombre vallée
L'ombre du grand Roland n'est donc pas consolée !
—Alfred de Vigny.

III

THE SONG OF ROLAND

ANYONE who walks through the Italian quarter of
New York City in the evening may notice over a door-
way an illuminated sign, THEATER OF MARIONETTES.
If his curiosity tempts him inside, into the low room
crowded with enthusiastic spectators, he will see, on
a rude stage, a group of puppets almost as large as
life, representing knights and ladies, acting out a little
drama in response to the jerking of strings fastened
to their arms and iron rods firmly fixed in their heads.
The warriors are gorgeously attired in shining armor
and plumed helmets, and the ladies have wonderful
costumes of bright colors, with a great deal of embroidery and decoration. An Italian in his shirt-sleeves,
half-concealed in the "wings" at the side of the stage,
speaks their lines for them, with all the elocutionary
flourishes which he can command. Fiercely immobile
as to expression, but most active as to arms and legs,
these manikins march about, soliloquize, make love,
and debate in council. But it is their battles which
arouse the greatest enthusiasm among the audience,
and indeed these are fought in a way that is a joy
to see. Then it is that heroic deeds are done, —
tin swords resound upon tin armor, helmets are bat-
tered about and knocked off, dust rises from the field,

the valiant dead fall in staring heaps. At such moments the spectators can hardly restrain themselves
for emotion, yet the story itself is well known to them,
— perhaps some one sitting near by will volunteer to
explain it, asserting that he has known it ever since he
was a boy, and that he has read it all in a book which
he has at home called the 'Reali di Francia.' It is a
version of the old tale of Charlemagne and his knights,
which, after traveling far from its native home in France,
was taken up by the Italian people many centuries ago,
and made so much their own that few heroes have been
closer to their hearts than Roland, or as they call him,
Orlando. Even in their homes in the New World they
still celebrate him, so that the very newsboys in the
streets of modern America are keeping alive the heroic
traditions of the age of Charlemagne.

No story illustrates better than this the popularity
of heroes of the Middle Ages in other countries than
their own. We have already observed, in considering
'Beowulf,' how Germanic worthies were welcomed,
irrespective of their nationality, wherever the fame of
their exploits had spread. And so it was in later days;
Charlemagne and Roland conquered the hearts of the
people of Germany, Italy, Spain, Scandinavia, and
England, just as the victorious armies of the French
were fabled to have left little of Western Europe un-
subdued. The accounts of their prowess were much
altered, it is true, in foreign countries. The Italians
provided Roland with many new and strange adventures, and took care that he should have plenty of
experience in love-making. The Germans conceived
him differently, sometimes emphasizing his devotion to

religion, sometimes seeing in his burly figure an embodiment of civic virtue. In some of the older towns of
Germany, as for example the old free city of Bremen,
there may be seen in the market-place or in some public
square a rude stone statue, fierce of expression, and
armed with a huge club. The name of this giant is
Roland, and he stands as a protector of the liberties
of the citizens, as a symbol of municipal justice. Still
more altered is the hero of the marionette shows in
America to-day. But we cannot be surprised at these
changes; the marvelous thing is that these old stories
have survived so long, and that the champion whom
they celebrate is, in a sense, as much alive to-day as he
ever was in legend. Neglected in his native France at
the present time, Roland seems assured of immortality
by his popularity in foreign lands.

This is all the more striking, since the tale of Roland
and Charlemagne was in the beginning a glorification
of the French, a triumphant outburst of French patriotism. No medieval story is more completely the expression of the ideals of a single nation. From beginning
to end, the 'Song of Roland' throbs with enthusiasm
for "sweet France," with ardent desire to advance her
fortunes, and to protect her from disgrace. It is
patriotism incarnate in verse. In a larger sense, the
ideals which the poem sets forth are not only those of
medieval times, but of the France of later centuries as
well, — ideals to which the nation owes much of its
glory. Even if the stirring old epic is no longer familiar
to the people of France as a whole, it breathes much
the same spirit which has animated them in great crises
of modern times. During the gloomy days of the

Franco-Prussian war which followed the disaster of Sedan, the great French scholar Gaston Paris saw hope for the future of his country in the persistence of its national idealism — a vision which was destined to brilliant fulfilment — and he illustrated his meaning by referring to this poem. "Two things are left us," he said, "of which, let us hope, nothing can deprive us, two of the three elements of the national idea in the 'Song of Roland,' — the love of the soil, of 'sweet France,' and the sentiment of national honor, in which we are all united." And it may be noted that one of the first great theatrical successes in Paris after the close of the war was Henri de Bornier's poetic drama, 'La Fille de Roland.'

In order fully to understand the spirit of the poem, we must remember that it is at once the epic of the eighth century and of the eleventh century. Its historical basis lies in the age of Charlemagne; its final development in the age of William the Conqueror. Under the sovereignty of Charlemagne, the Frankish people became the center of a truly imposing empire, extending on the north into what is now modern Germany, and on the south far into the Italian peninsula. They were successful not only in conquest, but also in gaining the support of the Church in maintaining and extending their power; the Pope himself crowned their king with solemn ceremonial as head of the Western Roman Empire, — afterwards that "Holy Roman Empire" which was to have such a strange history. This solidarity of the Franks in their own territories at home created among them a truly patriotic sentiment, while the magnificence of their domains abroad aroused among them a national pride, such as had never developed among the Germanic peoples who had sung of the deeds of Beowulf. Even after the disruption of the vast empire of Charlemagne, this proud consciousness of national glory still persisted; the State as such did not go out of existence completely, nor was there lack of reverence for the kingly power, sanctioned and confirmed as it was by Divine authority. The accidents of political change could not wholly destroy a heroic tradition. The persistence of this feeling of national unity is well illustrated in the 'Song of Roland,' which was mainly developed, not during the glorious days of the Carolingian empire, but in the time of its disruption, when the power of the king was small, and that of the nobles was great. Although it rests upon the historical traditions of the former age, and is informed with much of its spirit, the earliest and best version of it extant dates from the end of the eleventh century, and the political and social ideals which it sets forth are in large measure those of that period.

Tradition has it that the French marched into battle at Hastings listening to the recital of the deeds of Charlemagne and his knights from the lips of a minstrel named Taillefer. As the old chronicler puts it: —

> Taillefer spoke well indeed,
> Mounted on a coursing steed,
> Singing in the ducal train
> Of Roland and of Charlemagne,
> Of Oliver and many a brave vassal
> Who lost his life at Roncesvalles.

And Taillefer begged Duke William of Normandy, as the chronicler goes on to relate, that he might have the

privilege of striking the first blow in the ensuing battle.
The 'Song of Roland,' then, which rang out in the very
forefront of the advancing Norman host, may well stand
for the new French element added to the English people
by the Conquest, just as 'Beowulf' may represent the
older Germanic elements, Anglo-Saxon and Scandinavian, which had formerly dominated the island. Later,
in the legends of Arthur and his knights, we shall see the
influence of a still more brilliant and imposing France,
giving to the surrounding nations the refinements of
the developed system of chivalry, and the culture of
a gentler age. But we must not be unduly dazzled by
the magnificence of the later period. The contribution
of earlier days was less ornamental, but more enduring.

It is often said that it was most fortunate for the
English that the Normans were victorious in the battle
of Hastings. The vigor and enterprise of the French,
who were then just coming into prominence in Western
Europe, were just the qualities of which the island race
stood most in need. The glory of the Saxons was over;
they had for years been distracted by internal dissen-
sions, and disheartened by the rule of a Scandinavian
people, who had long been their enemies. Had William
the Conqueror never crossed the Channel, and set up
his standard on British soil, the future of the English
would indeed have been far different. But the new
ideals which were brought in by William and his followers, ideals of a young and ardent nation, combining
with the sterling qualities of the native Saxon stock,
produced, in the fullness of time, a race second in
distinction to none in Europe. The union of the two
peoples was like the marriage of a medieval monarch

and a captive princess of a stranger folk. Subdued in
the beginning completely to the power of the conqueror,
the mother-race asserted herself in later times by trans-
mitting her own characteristics to the children born of
this union.

We sometimes think of the Norman Conquest as the
invasion of an alien people. The new-comers spoke a
different tongue from the English, they were unlike them
in manners and in social organization, and they made
war after a different fashion. Yet it must not be forgotten that they were really of the same Germanic stock,
that the Normans who invaded England were so named
because they were descendants of the Northmen, the
Scandinavians, men of the same race who had in the
beginning celebrated the valor of Beowulf, before the
Anglo-Saxons perpetuated his fame in their epic. These
Northmen came to settle in what is now modern France
only about a century and a half before Duke William
sailed for the shores of England on his voyage of conquest. Other Frenchmen, some of whom went over
with him, or followed later, were likewise of German
extraction, — the Burgundians, for example, who had
once lived on the banks of the Rhine. It is there that
they dwell in the 'Nibelungenlied' and in the great
'Ring of the Nibelungen' music-dramas of Richard
Wagner. We realize the singular fact that the French
people are partly of German origin when we remember
that the very name "France" is derived from a German people, the Franks, who had once lived far north
of the present boundary between the two countries.
Ultimately these various tribes were fused with the
older Gallo-Romanic population, and thus modern

France came into being.   The incoming peoples adopted
the language of their new homes, just as their descendants were later to do in the British Isles.

This dualism of national origin produced no effect
upon the sentiment of unity which permeates the 'Song
of Roland.'   The fusion of the different elements in
the French people brought with it, indeed, a patriotism
so intense as to seem too self-centered.   In 'Beowulf'
the interest is confined to no one people, and the folk
of various lands are duly praised; in the 'Roland,' on
the other hand, the French are the undisputed heroes,
and no other Christian peoples are worth mentioning.
If we hear a good deal about the Saracens, it is not because the exploits of the Saracens are in themselves remarkable, but because the French warriors must have
worthy adversaries in order to exhibit their own valor.
In this lack of interest in other nations the 'Roland'
stands in sharp contrast to 'Beowulf,' and yet there is
much to suggest the fundamental kinship of the two
poems, and to remind us that the ideals of the French
epic are rooted in Germanic as well as in Romanic
customs.

The opening scenes of 'Beowulf' reveal the magnificence of a royal court of the earlier period, in a great
mead-hall filled with feasting warriors and echoing to
the strains of the harp and the clear voice of the minstrel.   The 'Song of Roland,' too, shows us a great
monarch surrounded by his nobles and retainers, but
the picture is far different.   Here there is no murky
northern twilight, with the sinister mists of the evening hanging over the haunted dunes by the seashore;
Charlemagne holds his court in the brilliant sunshine

of Southern Europe, out of doors, for he is absent from
home on a campaign in Spain. The royal throne, made
all of beaten gold, is placed beneath a pine tree; the
knights sit about the grass on cloths of white silk.
Some amuse themselves by playing games, others by
exercising with swords. In this bright and pleasant
scene there is little suggestion of the tragedy to come.
The Emperor is glad at heart, for he has been successful
in his long campaign of seven years against the "Saracens"; he has subdued all Spain, save only Saragossa,
in which King Marsilie is intrenched. And now the
pagan monarch, driven to desperation by continued
reverses, has sent a treacherous embassy to Charlemagne,
promising many things if the French will consent to
abandon their campaign in Spain. With olive branches
in their hands, the emissaries arrive at the Christian
camp, and deliver their message to the venerable king
as he sits beneath the pine. "No need have they to
ask which is the Emperor." On the following day,
the barons are summoned to a council to consider the
Saracen overtures. Count Roland advises against the
acceptance of these offers, reminding the assembly of the
tragic fate of two French envoys who were sent on a
previous occasion when the pagans had sued for peace.
His advice is that the war shall be waged to the bitter
end, and past injuries be avenged. But Ganelon, his
stepfather, urges the contrary, pointing out that pride
should not decide the issue, and that boastful speech
should have no weight. And his counsel is adopted;
the Saracen proposals are accepted. But who shall
carry this message back to the pagan king? No safe
or pleasant errand will this be, for, as Roland has said,

the men who had undertaken a similar errand were brutally murdered. Roland offers to go, and so does his friend and comrade Oliver, but Charlemagne will not listen to their proposals. Then on a sudden Roland says, "Let it be Ganelon, my stepfather."

The French say, "He will do this service well; if ye leave him out of account, ye will send no wiser man." Then said the King, "Ganelon, come thou forward, and receive the staff and the glove. Thou hast heard, the French have chosen thee." "Lord," said Ganelon, "it is Roland who has done all this; never again in my life shall I love him, nor Oliver, since he is his companion, nor the Twelve Peers, because they are devoted to him. In thy sight, Lord, I defy them all!"

Here we have the beginning of the tragic complications. Roland and his stepfather hate each other, it is clear. Step-relations have never agreed any better in story than in real life. Moreover, Roland increases Ganelon's anger to white heat by scornful jesting. And so Ganelon rides down into the paynim city in a towering rage, and on the way promises the ambassador of King Marsilie to betray his country for the satisfaction of his revenge and for riches. Arrived at the Saracen court, he advises the king to feign submission to Charlemagne, and then fall on his army as he retreats from Spain, and so to destroy the rear-guard, when it is divided from the main host. In this section of the army he plans to arrange that Roland shall be placed. So indeed it turns out. Ganelon returns to the French, announces that peace has been concluded, and completes his traitorous schemes. The Emperor is troubled with bad dreams, omens of disaster, but he withdraws from Spain, leaving behind only the rear-guard, containing the flower of his chivalry.   Meanwhile the pagans gather for the attack.

The next scene is a battle-piece, a long and elaborate description of the bloody conflict in the defiles of the Pyrenees.   "High are the hills and dark the valleys," but Oliver, the friend of Roland, ascending a mountain, sees in the distance the glitter of armor, and knows it is the heathen advancing against the French.   He urges his comrade to sound his horn, and summon the Emperor to their assistance.   But Roland refuses; he will not ask for help.

Oliver climbs a high mountain, and looks off to the right into a grassy valley, and he sees the army of the pagans advancing.   He calls to Roland his companion, " From Spain I see a great mass of armed men, of glittering hauberks and flaming helmets.   Great injury will they do to our band of Frenchmen.   Ganelon the traitor hath betrayed us; it was he who assigned us to the rear-guard, in the presence of the Emperor."   " Be silent, Oliver," answers Count Roland, " he is the husband of my mother, I would have you speak no word against him." . . . Says Oliver, " The pagans have a mighty host, and small indeed seems the number of our French soldiers.   Comrade Roland, sound thy horn!   Charles will hear it and the French will return."   Roland answers, " Folly would that be; all honor should I lose in sweet France.   Great blows will I strike with Durendal; the blade of the sword shall be covered with blood even unto the golden hilt.   In an evil hour for them have the pagans come into these mountain passes.   I warrant thee, they shall soon be dead men!"

Then the conflict begins, and the French and the Saracens fight a series of fearful hand-to-hand combats, but the overwhelming pagan force, four hundred thousand strong, is too much for the twenty thousand French warriors.   Finally, after appalling slaughter, Roland at last resolves to blow the horn and summon assistance, and with a mighty effort sounds a long peal, so loud and clear that the Emperor hears it in the distance, and turns back. But he comes too late; while he hastens southward, the French of the rear-guard are all slain, Roland only remaining alive. He too is near death, for the effort of sounding the horn has burst his temples. So he lies down beneath a pine tree and he dies, first vainly endeavoring to break his sword Durendal, that no pagan may bear it after his death.

Count Roland has laid him down beneath a pine tree, towards Spain has he turned his face. Many things he calls to memory, — all the lands which he has conquered as a warrior, and sweet France, the men of his kindred and Charlemagne his lord, who fostered him as a youth. He cannot restrain his sighs and his tears. But of himself he would not be forgetful, he confesses his sins and prays unto God for mercy, — "Our Father, who never hast deceived mankind, who hast raised up Lazarus from the dead and protected Daniel from the lions, save and defend thou my soul against all perils to which the sins I have done in my past life have exposed it!" In his right hand he lifts up his glove to heaven, and St. Gabriel receives it. Then the head of Roland sinks upon his arm, and with clasped hands he dies. God sends down his cherubim, and St. Michael of the Peril of the Seas, and together with them comes St. Gabriel. And they carry the soul of the count into Paradise.

The main theme of all this is plainly Valor, and not so much the valor of one man alone, as in 'Beowulf,' although Roland engages the chief interest, but of the whole French army. In the terrible hours in the pass of Roncesvalles, Roland is no more distinguished for his courage than are any of the rest; he is only a more formidable champion. The achievements of his companions are always treated with the greatest respect, and they are severally described in detail. Every one is a fighter, even the Archbishop Turpin, with his fair white hands, who girds himself up like the medieval Popes, and swinges mightily the enemies of God. The poet of the Anglo-Saxon epic seldom assigns any prominent part to those surrounding the hero. Beowulf, like the Turk, bears no brother near the throne. We do not think of the band of picked warriors who accompanied him to Denmark when he slew Grendel as his equals; his imposing figure hides them from view, and little is said of their exploits. Not so with the comrades of Roland. The Twelve Peers of France are the equals of the greater hero in everything but the possession of surpassing might; their courage is as high as his, and they are fully worthy to share his glory. In this drama there are many important characters, who play their parts nobly; the principal figure has no monopoly of the stage.

The whole evolution of the story, too, is different from that of 'Beowulf.' The Anglo-Saxon epic grew up by the addition of history to fairy-tales. The French story has developed from actual historical events. These have, it is true, been almost completely transformed, but they are, nevertheless, in the last analysis, real occurrences. In short, 'Beowulf' represents imagination modified by history; 'Roland' represents history modified by imagination. It must always be remembered that each epic has passed through many transmutations, in oral transmission, and that these are not merely matters of external decoration, but of plot and structure as well. When all elaborations have been removed, when due allowance has been made for all changes, and when the bare skeleton of historical fact which supports the whole stands revealed, we cannot but be astonished at the transformation of such a tiny acorn of truth into such a mighty oak of epic. There was once a combat in the Pyrenees, in which the rear-guard of Charlemagne's army, which was guarding the baggage-train, was attacked and routed with great slaughter. One of the officers who was killed was "Hruodlandus," governor of the March of Brittany. With the exception of a few details, and the remark that it was impossible to take immediate vengeance upon the enemy, this is practically all that history has to say about the main incident of the epic. Roland does not seem to have been more distinguished than other officers; in one early account he is not mentioned at all, and in the chief authority, the 'Life of Charlemagne' by Eginhard, he is only one of the leaders of the French, and he is mentioned last of the three. The whole affair was an episode, not a great national calamity, but it took such a hold upon the imagination of the people that it was magnified entirely out of its true proportions, and altered in whatever ways appeared to increase its interest and significance. Historically there was no treason, no Ganelon as stepfather and traitor, Roland was not the nephew of Charlemagne, and the combat was not with the Spanish Mohammedans, or "Saracens," as the poem styles them, but with the Basque mountaineers. It was, in all probability, much like a sharp guerilla attack. The marauding Basques of the Pyrenees were chiefly intent upon robbing the baggage of Charlemagne's army, hence they fell upon the French army in the rear, when it was forced to advance in dispersed formation, on account of the difficulties of the journey.

After the engagement was over, they crept back to their hiding-places, where it was impossible to reach them. Historically there was no glorious revenge, as in the epic. All the magnificence of the story as we read it in the Old French, all the pomp and circumstance of war, the burnished armor, the waving pennons, the flashing swords, the jeweled helmets, the golden-bossed shields, the serried ranks of armed men, — all this is a growth of later times. It is a part of the same tendency which makes Charlemagne over two hundred years old, whereas as a matter of fact he was probably younger than Roland. The epic loves the contrast between the venerable king, his beard sweeping like a mass of white flowers over his breast, and the sturdy and impetuous young hero, and so it rearranges history for the sake of that effect.

These changes, we must remember, are due not to the caprice of an individual author, but to the imagination of many different men, who have altered the story, not in writing, with a view to literary effect, but orally, with the aim of making the whole more heroic, more worthy to celebrate a great hero sprung from a mighty race. The traditions of still earlier times than the reign of Charlemagne may have assisted in this development; an occurrence in the reign of Dagobert, in which a Frankish army appears to have been surprised in the passes of the Pyrenees, may well have been fused in the popular imagination with the recollection of the disaster at Roncesvalles. But more important than such shadowy reminiscences of forgotten days are the elaborations made in the centuries following. The fascination of the wild mountain scenery, the treacherous attack, the desperate defense against a dangerous foe, the heroism

of warriors faithful to their trust, have inspired alterations which are magnificent, yet seldom grandiose.
Everything has been represented as of heroic proportions, that it may be in keeping with the heroism of the
action.   There is a certain large simplicity about it all,
which prevents exaggeration from degenerating into
grotesqueness.   Yet, as in so much popular poetry, — the
ballads, for example, — there is little variety of description; the same conventional terms are repeatedly applied to various persons or situations.   There is nothing
in the 'Roland' worthy to stand beside the lines in 'Beowulf' which portray the horror of the haunted mere in
the forest where Grendel and his dam abide.   The
French epic, though far later in date, is really far more
archaic in style, far less touched with romantic imagination.

A story such as this could not, of course, end with the
defeat of the French; it would have been intolerable to
leave the enemy in full satisfaction of their treasonable
victory.   So the third and concluding section narrates
the swift and terrible vengeance of Charlemagne, who
turns back the moment that he hears the horn of Roland reëchoing in the distant mountain passes. A
miracle is wrought for him; the sun stays its course in the
heavens that he may have light to overtake the Saracens.
First he annihilates such of them as he can find, and then
meets the greater host of the pagans and their allies.
This is no unequal combat, the fighting is long-continued,
but the pagans are finally routed, and their king, Marsilie, dies miserably of grief.   Saragossa is taken, and
the Emperor returns to France.   Ganelon the traitor is
tried, and after a judicial duel, is condemned to death.

Terrible is his end; wild horses tear him limb from limb, his bright blood flows out over the green grass. A strange contrast is this to the opening scene, the orchard decorated with white silk spread on the grass beneath the trees, and filled with a joyous and noble company, suspecting no evil. Now, at the end of the poem, many a goodly knight has fallen, sorrow and mourning fill the court, and the warriors who remain stand with stern faces and watch the bloody epilog to the tragedy.

It is not enough that the defeat of the French in the pass of Roncesvalles should be ascribed to superior numbers; popular imagination has further explained it as due to treachery. It is easy to see, however, that this must be very carefully managed, or else it will appear that the French are a race who may easily be guilty of treason, a worse reproach than being defeated in battle. Much depends upon the motive which prompts the traitor Ganelon to betray the French. As we have seen, this motive is undoubtedly, in the main, hatred of Roland. No explanation of this dislike is necessary; it is one of the constantly recurring motives of popular story. We all remember how many crimes were committed in fairy-tales by the stepmother, the *wicked* stepmother, as she is commonly called. Roland is meant to have the sympathy in this tale, just as stepchildren always do. But the fault does not seem to be all on Ganelon's side. It is clear that Roland has no love for his stepfather, and he certainly shows his distrust in an unmistakable way. In the council he mocks him with stinging words, and he proposes him for the dangerous mission to the Saracen court. It is hard to believe that Roland's motive was to do honor to his

mother's husband. At all events, Ganelon thinks that
Roland desires to get rid of him, and so plans, by destroying the rear-guard, to avenge himself on his stepson.

It seems likely, however, that in some forms of the
story the treason of Ganelon may have been attributed
to avarice. He is magnificently rewarded by the pagan
king; each year he is to have ten mules laden with the
finest gold of Arabia. On the battlefield Roland exclaims to Oliver, "Sir comrade, thou didst speak the
truth in saying that Ganelon hath betrayed us, and hath
received, as a reward for this, gold and silver and mer-
chandise." And again he says, "King Marsilie hath
bought and sold us." It must be remembered that a
story like this, circulating among the people in oral form,
told over and over again, was so much altered in the
course of time that even the motivation of the events
might be altered too. So the treason of Ganelon might
now be explained as due to avarice, and now as due
to vengeance. Then, when an epic was later made out
of such tales, both of these explanations might be preserved. The poet of the 'Song of Roland' seems to
have known different forms of the story, and not to
have hesitated to utilize both, even though they appeared contradictory. Thus in one passage he placed
Charlemagne's capital at Aix, and in another at Laon.
So he may well have taken something from more than
one version of the story in explaining the treason of
Ganelon. We have already noted a similar case in
'Beowulf,' where the fight with the dragon was attributed now to the hero's desire to possess the hoard of
treasure, and again to his resolve to protect his people
from a devastating scourge. The more closely popular

stories are examined, the more frequently do such incon-
sistencies as these appear. Consequently it is impossible to discuss the motivation in the 'Song of Roland'
as we should in a modern work of art.

If the principal motive of Ganelon's treachery in the
poem as we read it to-day is desire for revenge, does this
in any way serve to excuse the crime? Was treason on
the part of a Frenchman less dishonorable if prompted
by vengeance? Nowadays, in the twentieth century,
we should answer that it was not; but a man of the
eleventh century would have thought differently. In
early times very great importance was attached to revenge; it was no mere gratification of spite; it was a
sacred duty, one of the most pressing of all social obli-
gations. Injuries inflicted upon one's own person or
property, or upon the lives or possessions of his kinsmen,
could be satisfied only by the infliction of equal or greater
damage upon the guilty party. If a man was killed,
the murderer might settle the affair with the dead man's
relatives by paying them a sum of money, otherwise it
was their duty to slay him. We can hardly realize
what a stain lay upon family honor until such an affair
was settled. The conflict between revenge and other
duties or passions is of course one of the commonest
motives in early poetry. It forms the theme of the greatest tragedy in English literature, which may be read, in
crude but unmistakable form, in a Latin history of the
Danes written only a little later than the present version
of the 'Roland.' The gentle Hamlet and the boorish
Amlethus ultimately are really one and the same. It
was a peculiarly bitter reproach to the warriors of Hrothgar, in 'Beowulf,' that they could not be avenged upon

Grendel for all his injuries, nor could they expect that he would atone for the death of their kinsmen by the payment of money. And so Ganelon feels that he must "get even" with Roland. In the presence of Charlemagne and all the barons he utters his formal defiance; he warns Roland, as it were, that vengeance is to follow.

"Lord," said Ganelon, "it is Roland who has done all this; never again in my life shall I love him, nor Oliver, since he is his companion, nor the Twelve Peers, because they are devoted to him. In thy sight, Lord, I defy them all!"

This forms Ganelon's defense, when, at the end of the story, he is tried for high treason.

" I defied Roland the warrior, and Oliver, and all their comrades; and Charles and all his noble barons were witnesses of this. I have revenged me, but in that there is no treason."

Thus, according to the customs of the time, Ganelon was, in one sense, acting within his rights. At his trial the barons are even disposed to pardon him, but Charlemagne is anxious for his conviction, because Roland is his nephew, his blood-relation, and he must have vengeance upon his murderer. This desire is at length satisfied; one of the barons points out that Ganelon is a traitor because he has broken his oath of allegiance to the Emperor, a more binding obligation than the duty of compassing personal revenge.

"Whatever wrong Roland may have done to Ganelon, he was in thy service, and that should have afforded him protection. Ganelon is a felon in that he has betrayed him, and hath broken his oath unto thee, and hath done evil. And therefore I vote for his death; let him be hanged, and let his body be cast out to the dogs as that of a felon and a traitor. If any kinsman he hath who will give me the lie in this, I stand ready to defend my judgment with the sword which I have girded here at my side."

And so, in accordance with the medieval fashion of deciding points of law by fighting them out, in the belief that God will make the right side victorious, a judicial duel between one of Ganelon's kinsmen and a champion of Charlemagne takes place. Ganelon's guilt is established by the defeat of his defender, so he is put to death, and his kinsmen with him. Thus, in this epic which exalts the virtue of the French, the treason of Ganelon is partially excused. He is a traitor, but his crime is mitigated by the fact that he has been obliged to choose between conflicting duties, — the satisfaction of vengeance and allegiance to the Emperor.

The tragedy in the pass of Roncesvalles is thus, in the last analysis, partly the fault of Roland himself. Had he not uttered insulting words to his stepfather, had he not proposed him for a dangerous and possibly fatal mission, Ganelon's dreadful revenge would never have been planned. Even granting that he had no sinister motive in suggesting Ganelon as ambassador to the Saracens, his act points to the same fatal defect in his character which leads him to dismiss all prudence in the face of danger. His reckless impetuosity always carries him away; his resolution soars so high that he never stops to think of consequences. In the most extreme danger he scorns to sound his horn for aid, preferring to sacrifice many lives to a rather theatrical heroism. Such reckless bravado was, of course, a tradition of the age, as it is more or less of all ages in which military achievement is the controlling ideal. Germanic warriors went to certain death, even when no great end was to be gained thereby, rather than compromise with valor for the sake of safety. The

Niblungs, though forewarned, faring to the court of Attila, or the kinsmen of Signy accepting the treacherous invitation of King Siggeir, were doing no more than flesh and blood heroes were wont to do. Hamthir and Sörli press alone into the halls of Eormanric, and perish with the words, "What though we die? Glory awaits us!" There is much about Roland that recalls Shakspere's Hotspur, — a figure which has a fascination, in its complete abandon to heroic impulse, which is somewhat lacking in the more cautious Prince Hal. But it is noteworthy that in the 'Song of Roland' the claims of reason and common-sense are given a chance against splendid and reckless folly. These are represented in the person of Oliver, Roland's friend and companion in arms. He is as brave as Roland, but of better balanced character; he stops to think. The poem contrasts the two in a pithy phrase: "Roland is brave, and Oliver is wise." Oliver is only a secondary figure, he is by no means the perfect embodiment of valor which we see in Roland, and he pales before the glory of his more illustrious comrade. But Oliver points out that Roland's blind heroism and reckless striving for honor may result in actual dishonor. When both are far spent on the battlefield, Oliver exclaims: —

"Comrade, the fault is thine. Wise valor is not rashness, and prudence is better than recklessness. Through thine imprudence the French have met their end; nevermore can we render service unto Charles the King. Hadst thou hearkened unto me, he would have come, and we should have won this battle, and King Marsilie would have been killed or captured. O Roland, an evil thing hath thy prowess been for us! Charles the Great shall nevermore have assistance from thee, and never until the day of doom will there be another man such as thou art. Die thou must, *and France shall thereby be put to shame*."

In order fully to appreciate the spirit of the poem, we must look with particular care at Charlemagne. He is, in a sense, an imaginary monarch, he is idealized out of all historical reality, but these very idealizations represent the conception of kingship in the minds of the people. He is first of all majestic, his whole presence breathes authority; he has the dignity of great age, symbolized by the white beard which flows over his breast. He has been a mighty warrior, having subdued most of the kingdoms of earth, so that he represents, in the second place, kingly valor. He is politically supreme, but he does not use his power despotically. In councils he has the deciding voice, but his barons advise rather than legislate; "he wishes to do nothing without those of France." In the greater council or court of justice which tries Ganelon for high treason he is only the presiding officer. He is head of the Church as well as of the State; not only sovereign but patriarch. He has direct communication with Heaven, and is protected by a special guardian angel. And yet, despite his imposing personality, there is a pathos about his figure. In his old age he is obliged to lose the bravest of his warriors in the disaster at Roncesvalles, and even after he has avenged the slain, he has little peace. The poem opens with his triumph; it ends with his despair. As soon as the execution of Ganelon is over, he is summoned to aid the Christians in a distant land.

The king lies down to sleep in his vaulted chamber. But St. Gabriel comes to him from God and says to him, "Charles, collect the armies of thine empire, and go in full power into the land of Bire, and aid King Vivien at Imphe, at the city which the pagans have besieged ; the Christians call unto thee for succor." The Emperor would fain not have gone. "Ah God !" he cries, "how full of troubles is my life !" And he weeps, and plucks his white beard.

The very sorrows which afflict Charlemagne make him still more impressive. He stands in lonely grandeur, — the incarnation of imperial piety, valor, and dominion.

The 'Song of Roland' was shaped by the hands of many men; it was the work of the French people in different parts of the country, not in one district alone; it is truly a national epic. It appears to have been influenced only in a small degree, if at all, by ecclesiastics, and yet no saint's life, no Bible story, shows greater religious fervor. "For God and sweet France !" — this is the cry which rings through it all, and even sweet France takes the second place. But it unites very closely both patriotic and religious conceptions. It proclaims not only that all Frenchmen are Christians, but also that all Christians are Frenchmen. As the poet of another old song says: —

> The crown of France must be exalted,
> For all other kings should be subject to it, —
> All such as believe in God and the law of Christendom.

The old Germanic belief was that you ought to fight your neighbors, and if necessary exterminate them, for the glory of arms. The belief of the French in the 'Song of Roland' is that you ought to exterminate them anyhow, provided they are not Christians, and if they are you ought to annex them. The matter is very simple. "Christians are right, and pagans are wrong," says the poet. So the wars in the 'Roland' are really religious contests, like the Crusades, and the epic, with its intense and narrow piety, makes us understand the fanatical enthusiasm which inspired expeditions to the Holy Land. It points forward to the First Crusade, which took place not long after the poem assumed its present shape. Its religion suggests rather a primitive type of Christianity, — God is a kind of heavenly Charlemagne, a being not unlike the Emperor, only still more remote and powerful. Yet the God of Roland is not really so far off as the God of Beowulf. In the Anglo-Saxon epic, as we have seen, the Deity interferes little in the main action, and the issue is decided by the strength of the hero. But the God of Charlemagne is willing to stop the very sun in the heavens for the benefit of the French. This Beowulf would have considered an unsportsmanlike advantage; he always fought fair, even against demons. But he was only vaguely pious, whereas the French warriors are completely and sincerely devoted to the service of their God.

Women play but a small part in this heroic story. The soldiers returning from the wars think of their wives and sweethearts, but Roland quite forgets the lovely Aude, his affianced bride, the sister of Oliver. She does not forget him, however. The moment that the Emperor returns to his capital, she runs to him to hear news of Roland.

The Emperor returns from Spain and comes to Aix, the fairest city of France; he enters the palace and advances into the great hall. Unto him comes Aude, a damsel radiant in beauty, who says to him, "Where is Roland the captain, who hath plighted me his troth to take me as his wife?" Charles is filled with sorrow and grief, he weeps, and plucks his white beard. "Sister, sweet friend, thou askest me of a dead man. But in exchange for Roland will I give thee Louis, a better know I not in France. My son he is, and will govern my dominions." Aude answers, "Strange are thy words; may it not please God or his saints or angels that I should live after Roland's death!" The color fades from her face, she falls at the feet of Charlemagne, she is dead! May God have mercy on her soul!

Bramimonde, the Saracen queen, is a devoted wife; not a lovely fragile flower, like Aude, but able to speak her mind vigorously on occasion. Her soul was worth saving; at first she refused to accept Christianity, but "having heard many sermons and examples," was at length won over. In the *chansons de geste* ladies generally get more consideration than their lords and masters, and are given a chance to embrace the true faith, and live happily ever after, sometimes as the brides of their conquerors. But in this poem, which was unaffected by the development of romantic conventions, the presence of women arouses little interest, and has little effect on the dramatic action. The love-element has not yet become vital in heroic narrative. It has indeed been conjectured that the whole episode dealing with Aude is really extraneous, possibly a separate lyric which has been worked into the fabric of the epic, and which reveals its incongruity with the spirit of the poem as a whole.

Like 'Beowulf,' the 'Song of Roland' glorifies the ruling aristocracy. Royal and noble personages are again the actors, and little attention is paid to those of inferior rank. The people are vaguely in the background, but their fortunes arouse no interest. Twenty thousand French perish in the defiles of the Pyrenees, but the common soldiers are almost completely disregarded. The epic avoids whatever is not magnificent,

— even in describing the four hundred thousand pagans, it mentions only "counts and viscounts, dukes and almaçurs and emirs and sons of counts." Only rarely do the lower classes make their appearance, as when, in a passage of rough humor, the cooks of Charlemagne's kitchen amuse themselves by tormenting the unhappy Ganelon, who has been given into their charge. But even then there must be no less than a hundred of them! When we compare the poem carefully with what has gone before, we cannot but feel a change in the relations of men to each other. While there is not yet the intense caste-feeling of the later Middle Ages, there is less of the democratic spirit about this society than about that described in 'Beowulf.' Rank has assumed added importance, and pride of birth shows signs of its later transformation into the intolerance of the fully developed system of chivalry.

"The *chansons de geste* are fine specimens of fighting Christianity," says Lowell, "but who after reading them —even the best of them, the 'Song of Roland'—can remember much more than a cloud of battle-dust, through which the paladins loom dimly gigantic, and a strong verse flashes here and there like an angry sword?"— Do we gain no more definite impression than this from the 'Song of Roland'? May we not carry away with us a vision of a people for whom fighting was indeed still the chief business of life, but who had progressed far enough to feel the beauty of devotion to a national ideal and of submission to a beneficent God? With all his headstrong impetuosity, with all his forgetfulness of consequences, Roland is far more unselfish than the warrior of Germanic times. His very folly springs from his own eager desire to advance the interests of his native country and to reflect glory upon his kin, as much as from his own warlike disposition. From the lips of the French hero might well have come the words which Macaulay made Horatius utter:—

> To every man upon this earth
> Death cometh soon or late;
> And how can man die better
> Than facing fearful odds,
> For the ashes of his fathers
> And the temples of his gods?

This broader vision, this consecration to a higher ideal of Church and State, which is the animating force behind all the tumult and carnage at Roncesvalles, and of which the heroism of Roland is the symbol, was not the least of those elements in the French character which, in spite of much that was selfish and sordid, quickened the life of the English into new vigor after the Conquest, and made possible their later achievement in the years to come.

IV

THE ARTHURIAN ROMANCES

I was first of all the kings who drew
The knighthood-errant of this realm and all
The realms together under me, their Head,
In that fair Order of my Table Round,
A glorious company, the flower of men,
To serve as model for the mighty world,
And be the fair beginning of a time.
I made them lay their hands in mine and swear
To reverence the King, as if he were
Their conscience, and their conscience as their King,
To break the heathen and uphold the Christ,
To ride abroad redressing human wrongs,
To speak no slander, no, nor listen to it,
To honor his own word as if his God's,
To lead sweet lives in purest chastity,
To love one maiden only, cleave to her,
And worship her by years of noble deeds.

— TENNYSON.

IV

THE ARTHURIAN ROMANCES

In one of his most whimsical moments, Mark Twain conceived the idea of placing a Connecticut Yankee at the court of King Arthur, and contrasting New England shrewdness and common-sense with medieval credulity and superstition. This daring bit of fancy he elaborated with inimitable humor. We all remember how the Yankee appeared at a tournament clad in the lightest of acrobatic attire, and then lassooed the iron-clad knights and pulled them off their horses in clattering heaps, how he discomfited Merlin by a liberal use of gunpowder, and saved himself from the stake by some remarkable astronomical calculations about an eclipse. Most ingenious, too, were his methods of calling attention to the merits of Persimmons's soap and Peterson's prophylactic tooth-brush. But while Mark Twain puts us in the best of humor by his fun, and arouses our interest by vivid and unconventional descriptions of Arthur and Guinevere and Launcelot and Kay and other worthies of the court, he is really bent on showing quite a different side of the picture. The Yankee looks about in the king's dominions, and sees poverty and squalor and suffering among the common people, cruelty and injustice in the great noblemen and heroes, wretchedness and vice beneath all the glitter of the Round Table fellowship. The domain

of King Arthur is made the symbol of the social shortcomings of the Middle Ages.   At the very beginning
of the story, the author reveals his true purpose.   The
Yankee goes up to Camelot as the prisoner of Sir Kay
the Seneschal : —

As we approached the town, signs of life began to appear.   At
intervals we passed a wretched cabin, with a thatched roof, and
about it small fields and garden patches in an indifferent state of
cultivation.   There were people, too ; brawny men, with long, coarse,
uncombed hair that hung down over their faces and made them look
like animals.   They and the women, as a rule, wore a coarse tow-
linen robe that came well below the knee, and a rude sort of sandals,
and many wore an iron collar. . . .   In the town were some substantial windowless houses of stone scattered among a wilderness
of thatched cabins ; the streets were mere crooked alleys, and
unpaved ; troops of dogs and nude children played in the sun
and made life and noise ; hogs roamed and rooted contentedly
about, and one of them lay in a reeking wallow in the middle
of the main thoroughfare and suckled her family.   Presently
there was a distant blare of military music ; it came nearer, still
nearer, and soon a noble cavalcade wound into view, glorious with
plumed helmets and flashing mail and flaunting banners and rich
doublets and horse-cloths and gilded spear-heads ; and through the
muck and swine, and naked brats, and joyous dogs, and shabby huts
it took its gallant way, and in its wake we followed.   Followed
through one winding alley and then another, — and climbing, always
climbing — till at last we gained the breezy height where the huge
castle stood.   There was an exchange of bugle blasts ; then a parley
from the walls, where men-at-arms in hauberk and morion marched
back and forth with halberd at shoulder under flapping banners
with the rude figure of a dragon displayed upon them ; and then the
great gates were flung open, the drawbridge was lowered, and the
head of the cavalcade swept forward under the frowning arches.

The sympathies of Mark Twain were always profoundly
stirred by injustice and inhumanity, and he seldom

dealt with bygone ages without reminding us of the misery of the unfortunate and the oppressed. 'The Prince and the Pauper' is almost as much an exposure of social conditions under Edward VI as it is a story; 'Joan of Arc' is full of pity for a noble woman struggling against overwhelming odds. Mark Twain was a great humorist, but he was also a great humanitarian.

His picture of medieval society is true, in a sense. In the twelfth and thirteenth centuries, when the Arthurian romances reached their greatest glory, the lower classes received little consideration; they often lived in wretchedness, and trembled under oppression. The pleasures of this world were not for them, but rather its sorrows and its burdens. This is really the era into which the Yankee is transported, this was the Age of Chivalry, although Mark Twain prefers to disguise it transparently as the sixth century, when the Arthur of history actually flourished. It is true, too, that the romances, the amusement and the expression of the upper classes, do not at all reflect the social condition of the people as a whole. They disregard the commons, in most cases, even more completely than the 'Song of Roland' does. Their tone is aristocratic throughout. They reveal the brighter side of medieval life, — love-affairs and tournaments and brilliant military expeditions and knightly deeds and romantic adventures, ignoring the peasantry toiling to pay tithes and taxes, falling unwept in battles made glorious by their superiors, dying of pestilence, suffering from the ravages of war, or perishing miserably of famine. Such things as these Mark Twain has chosen to bring

vividly before us, casting a heavy shadow over the brightness and beauty of Arthurian romance.

Yet the serious parts of his book are, I believe, profoundly misleading, despite the generosity of feeling
which has inspired them and the facts which may be
advanced to support them.   When the humorist lays
aside his cap and bells, and becomes the moralist, when
he uses the Arthurian romances as illustrations of the
defective social consciousness of the later Middle Ages,
he mistakes the true character of these romances, and
forgets the spirit which really underlies them.   They
voice the sentiments of a single class of society, indeed,
but one which, with all its faults, was slowly progressing
towards finer issues, — the gentleness, generosity, and
reverence for women, which were lacking in the Heroic
Age.   It is their idealism which has given the Arthurian
legends, in part at least, their wonderful vitality, making
the story of the Round Table heroes the most popular
of all the romantic narratives of the Middle Ages, and
attracting in modern times poets so unlike as Spenser
and Tennyson.   Even Milton, we remember, seriously
considered making King Arthur the bearer of the message which later came in the pages of 'Paradise Lost.'
We cannot afford to underestimate the literature of
idealism.   It is a trite saying that a period must be
judged not alone by literature which depicts things as
they are, but also by that which depicts things as men
would fain have them.   The plays of Shakspere are a
truer guide to the spirit of Elizabethan England than is
contemporary history; the French Revolution is illuminated by the works of the poets and novelists of the day
as much as by documentary annals; More's 'Utopia' is

hardly less history than Bacon's 'Henry the Seventh.'
So it is in the Middle Ages; Arthurian romance is the
'Utopia' of chivalry. It is unreal and fantastic; but it
represents a definite ideal of conduct. It even contains,
as we shall observe later, the beginnings of humanita-
rianism. Mark Twain failed to see, then, that he was
selecting as an illustration of the degradation of the
times a story which was really the herald of better conditions, and that in reproaching the Arthurian knights
for lack of human sympathy he was overlooking those
very efforts to establish finer social ideals, which, first
manifested by the members of the ruling aristocratic
class in their relations with each other, were in time extended to those of lower social station.

The adventures of Arthur and his knights were peculiarly adapted to become the concrete expression of
chivalric ideals, since they were almost wholly the product of imagination. In this regard they form a strong
contrast to the exploits of Roland and Charlemagne.
What the "matter of France" shows directly and real-
istically, the "matter of Britain" shows indirectly and
symbolically. In the representation of a perfect system of knighthood, Arthurian romance is undisturbed
by intruding facts of contemporary politics. Charlemagne, despite all the fantasy and exaggeration with
which his figure has been surrounded, is nevertheless
always the sovereign of a real empire, the ruler of France.
His deeds and those of his knights are to a considerable
extent founded on fact, and they are perhaps none the
less a part of the history of France because the French
people have altered them to suit their own conceptions.
Roland and Oliver were born of national struggle and

exalted by patriotic pride, and they still belonged to
the people at the time of their greatest glory in the 'Song
of Roland.' Three centuries after his death, Charlemagne could stand as representative of the French crown,
even though its struggles were then against baronial
power at home rather than against foes abroad. His
name and fame were still supreme in spite of changed
political conditions. For, in their eagerness to defend
his rebellious barons, poets of the later day did not hesitate to charge him with oppressions and iniquities. He
was frequently humiliated in the *chansons de geste* in
order that such insurgent heroes as Girart de Vienne
might be exalted. In short, he was real enough, even
after he had long been dead, to be affected by changes
in the political situation in France.

Not so with Arthur. While his story was, like Roland's, founded on stirring events in the history of a nation, and fostered in its infancy by patriotic pride, it
reached its fullest development among foreigners, who
loved it, in a sense, because of its very freedom from
disturbing political realities. The national element
quickly faded out; there was little Celtic enthusiasm in
the heyday of Arthurian romance. Nor did it achieve
a transferred patriotism. One does not imagine such
a phrase as "sweet France" on the lips of Launcelot or
Bedivere. The great king himself rules an imaginary
realm; he has little to do with the realities of politics,
domestic or international. As time goes on, he gets to
be more and more a shadowy and passive figure, and
the glory of other heroes sitting at the Round Table dims
the brightness of his own renown. But they are not
essentially different from him; Tristram and Perceval

and Gawain and the rest exist not to deliver the people of Britain from their enemies, but to rescue ladies and kill monsters, and to undergo wonderful adventures in love and war. They are warriors of fairyland, half enveloped in a golden haze of unreality. The ugly things of life occasionally intrude; but the treason of Mordred or the unfaithfulness of Guinevere spring from no necessity of rationalizing or explaining historical events, as in the case of the treachery of Ganelon, which is made to motivate the slaughter at Roncesvalles. It is unsafe, too, to attribute to such episodes a mythological origin. Arthur, who may fitly stand as representative of his whole court, is king of dreams and monarch of fantasy. His miraculous translation to Avalon is the only end possible for a career more suggestive of the otherworld than of a land of sordid realities. He is an ideal, "Arthur, flower of kings," as Joseph of Exeter called him, and the stories grouped around his name are really as imaginary as fairy-tales.

Arthurian romance is like a gorgeous tapestry, woven of many threads, and colored with many dyes. Some of the materials have come from distant countries, — here a bit of gold from the Orient, there a homespun strand of popular story, but the warp is Celtic and the woof is French. Much of the embroidery, too, is Celtic, and it is the Celtic coloring which gives the whole much of its charm, but, in vivid contrast to this, French workers have so disposed their own brilliant hues as to give harmony to a design, which, though striking, was in the beginning crude and archaic. The web and the embroidery were long in the making, — the longer, because so much was unraveled to make room for newer patterns, and because old designs were constantly elaborated afresh. We shall be mainly concerned here with the form which the romances assumed during the three centuries following the 'Song of Roland'; that is to say, from the Norman Conquest to the age of Chaucer. Even within this period changes are many, consistency is often lacking, absurdities and exaggerations creep in. Chaucer ridiculed the artificiality of the romances, and their straining of probabilities, as in

— the book of Launcelot de Lake,
That wommen holde in ful gret reverence.

Some heroes grow more illustrious; some, like Galahad, appear for the first time; and some are thrust completely into the background by the prestige of their newer rivals. Prose romances run to wearisome length; artistic form is neglected, or lost in a mass of detail. Vulgar story-tellers drag Arthur down into the dust of the highway, or make him the amusement of coarse wits in the ale-house. Monkish piety makes romance a vehicle for religion, or allegorizes a thumping moral into it. Nevertheless, in spite of its blemishes, Arthurian romance at the height of its chivalric period presents many striking characteristics which distinguish it from earlier and later conceptions. We shall best understand these characteristics if we first look at the origins of the legend as a whole, and then at some of the chief influences which have molded it.

At the beginning of the sixth century, the Celtic peoples in Britain, who had earlier welcomed the assistance of the Germanic tribes against their enemies, the Picts and Scots, were engaged in a series of desperate

struggles to check the encroachments of their former
allies. This was the era of the historical events recorded in 'Beowulf'; Hygelac was still king of the Geats,
and his disastrous expedition into the Low Countries
was yet to be undertaken. The task of the Celtic
peoples in attempting to preserve their liberties and
to retain their dominions was not easy. But in one
engagement, the Battle of Mons Badonis, or Mount
Badon, they were temporarily successful, under the
leadership of a certain Arthur, not their king, but the
commander of their forces. This victory, though it
really signified little for the ultimate outcome of the
struggle, gave a tremendous impetus to the formation
of heroic legends about the figure of Arthur. It was
perhaps inevitable that these legends should soon become a lament for a forlorn cause and a sigh for a lost
leader. The Celtic temperament is not primarily suited
to political achievement. Enthusiasm and imagination
do not make up for the lack of certain sterner virtues
which lead to success in establishing and governing a
state. Mommsen's characterization of the Celts at the
time of their early contact with the Romans holds for the
medieval period as well. "Nature," he says, "though she
lavished upon the Celts her most brilliant gifts, had denied
them those more solid and enduring qualities which lead
to the highest human development, alike in morality
and politics." So it is easy to understand the reverence
of the Celts for such of their leaders as have excelled
in practical affairs. To this reverence is due the genesis
of the legend of Arthur. He achieved renown as the
leader of his people in their hour of need, and his
successes instantly magnified his position. From being

so little distinguished that one of the early chroniclers does not even mention his name, he is presently invested with the dignity of a great epic hero, and his victories grow in number and in significance. In the Latin history of Nennius, a compilation of uncertain authorship and date, the traces of popular imagination are plainly to be seen. Arthur is said to have been successful in twelve battles, and to have slain nine hundred and forty of the enemy in the contest at Mount Badon. But his growing fame soon took other forms, some idea of which may be gained from the celebrated compilation of Welsh stories called the 'Mabinogion.' The narratives in this collection differ widely in provenience and date, but from those of more primitive form we may gain some idea of the Arthur of song and story while he was still a half-savage Celtic ruler. The exploits of his heroes, as related here, belong rather to old wives' tales than to the glories of romance. In character and appearance, too, these heroes are indeed different from the "flowers of courtesy" of a later age. Osla Gyllellvawr, one of his champions, bore a short broad dagger with the marvelous property that "when Arthur and his hosts came before a torrent, they would seek for a narrow place where they might pass the water, and would lay the sheathed dagger across the torrent, and it would form a bridge sufficient for the armies of the three Islands of Britain, and of the three islands adjacent, with their spoil." "Sgilti Yscawndroed, when he intended to go on a message for his Lord, never sought to find a path, but knowing whither he was to go, if his way lay through a wood he went along the tops of the trees." "Sugyn, the son of Sugnedydd . . . would suck up the sea on which were three hundred ships, so as to leave nothing but a dry strand." The haughty Kay of the later romances appears in this motley company, as outlandish, apparently, as the rest. "So great was the heat of his nature that, when it rained hardest, whatever he carried remained dry for a handbreadth above and a handbreadth below his hand; and when his companions were coldest, it was to them as fuel with which to light their fire." Some of these curious characteristics may be seen even in the pages of Sir Thomas Malory; Gawain's strength waxed and waned with the course of the day.

These more primitive tales in the 'Mabinogion' are not merely fantastic; they often prefigure the beauty and richness of the later romances. Kilhwch, the young warrior who, with the aid of Arthur, performs seemingly impossible feats in order to win his bride, appears before us in all the radiance of Celtic poetry.

The youth pricked forth upon a steed with head dappled grey, of four winters old, firm of limb, with shell-formed hoofs, having a bridle of linked gold on his head, and upon him a saddle of costly gold. And in the youth's hand were two spears of silver, sharp, well-tempered, headed with steel, three ells in length, of an edge to wound the wind, and cause blood to flow, and swifter than the fall of the dew-drop from the blade of reed-grass upon the earth when the dew of June is at the heaviest. A gold-hilted sword was upon his thigh, the blade of which was of gold, bearing a cross of inlaid gold of the hue of the lightning of heaven; his war-horn was of ivory. . . . And his courser cast up four sods with his four hoofs, like four swallows in the air, about his head, now above, now below. About him was a four-cornered cloth of purple, and an apple of gold was at each corner, and every one of the apples was of the value of an hundred kine. And there was precious gold of the value of three hundred kine upon his shoes, and upon his stirrups, from his knee to the tip of his toe. And the blade of grass bent not beneath him, so light was his courser's tread as he journeyed towards the gate of Arthur's palace.

About the middle of the twelfth century, Arthur first emerged definitely from his semi-barbaric Celtic surroundings, and, after a proper introduction to the world, entered the most fashionable society of Western Europe, and reorganized his court according to the most approved models. In those days, as for many centuries to come, France was the arbiter of taste in manners, dress, and fashions generally. Under the hands of the French, Arthur and his knights became accomplished courtiers, with all the graces of the age, clad in fair raiment, and with new refinements of thought and feeling. The Conquest was one means of bringing this about; the Anglo-French were fond of a good story, and saw in Arthur a champion not less interesting than their own heroes. Again, the peoples of Celtic stock in France itself, especially in Brittany or Armorica, had perpetuated the name and fame of Arthur among themselves, and they now added their contribution to French romance. Which of these two sources is mainly responsible for the astonishing spread of the story among the French is still a matter of dispute among scholars; but if we consider that each source had in all likelihood its due share, we need not trouble ourselves about the precise details. The celebrated Geoffrey of Monmouth did much to make the material popular among the French on English soil, by embodying it in his so-called "history." A historical novel we may better call it, or perhaps merely a novel, since imaginative and legendary incidents so far outweigh real facts. The important thing to note is that here Arthur is first drawn out of the Celtic twilight, invested with the magnificence of a medieval monarch, and introduced to the world at large. He is no longer served by "a red, rough, ill-favored man, having red whiskers with bristly hairs," as in the 'Dream of Rhonabwy' in the 'Mabinogion.' Such uncouth servitors are banished, and some of the "thousand young noblemen, all clothed in ermine," who attended him at his coronation are doubtless retained. In Geoffrey's pages Arthur and his court come up in the world mightily, with much of the elegance which was later to surround them as the ideal representatives of the system of chivalry. As Geoffrey says, "At that time Britain had arrived at such a pitch of grandeur, that in abundance of riches, luxury of ornaments, and politeness of inhabitants, it far surpassed all other kingdoms. The knights in it that were famous for feats of chivalry wore their clothes and arms all of the same color and fashion; and the women also no less celebrated for their wit, wore all the same kind of apparel, and esteemed none worthy of their love but such as had given proof of their valor in three several battles. Thus was the valor of the men an encouragement for the women's chastity, and the love of the women a spur to the soldiers' bravery."

We may compare with the cruder tales in the 'Mabinogion,' from which illustrations of the more primitive forms of the story have been cited, others in the same collection which have passed through the hands of the French and thus gained new elegance. The fact that the Welsh welcomed their own stories back again in a new dress, and gave them a place in one of the most

famous of all their collections of native narratives well
illustrates the influence exerted by France upon surrounding nations.   Practically all the Arthurian romances in English are either translated from French
originals or imitated from French models, and the same is
true, with some reservations, of the tales of the knights
of the Round Table in Germany and Italy and the
Scandinavian countries.   The greatest period of German poetry, aside from the era of Goethe and Schiller, —
the period of Wolfram von Eschenbach, and Hartmann
von Aue, and Gottfried von Strassburg, — would have
been impossible had it not been for French poets.   And
so, while we shall look to Germany for the most profoundly religious and symbolical version of the Legend
of the Holy Grail, and for the noblest conception of the
love of Tristram and Iseult, and to England for the most
refined conception of the courtesy of Gawain, we must
never forget that the fountain-head of the inspiration
which produced these masterpieces was French poetry.

It is interesting to imagine what Roland and Gawain
would have thought of each other had they met by
chance in their wanderings.   It seems probable that
while each would have paid due respect to the courage
of the other, Roland would have thought Gawain finicky
and sentimental, too much worried over detail, too elaborate in his manners, while Gawain would have felt Roland too rude and boastful, too lacking in consideration
for women and somewhat deficient in knightly courtesy.
Roland, we feel, would have more sympathy with Beowulf than with Gawain.   By birth and breeding Roland
belongs in the Heroic Period, albeit at its very close.
But when Gawain rides forth into the fields of European

romance, a new set of social laws has come into existence, without observance of which no manners at all are possible. We must now see just how these laws arose, and how they affected those aristocratic circles with which the Arthurian story is primarily concerned.

For the genesis of chivalry, which grew up coincidently with the fullest development of the feudal system, we must look rather to the south than to the north of France. The 'Song of Roland,' as we have seen, represents to a large extent the Germanic elements of the northern part of the country, those sterner virtues which led to success in war and made politics a matter of force. In the south, the Gallo-Latin element in the population produced a softer and more sensuous temperament, a greater devotion to the fragile and joyous and beautiful things of life. The very name Provence suggests the music of Troubadours and the smiles of women. The north was a region of deeds, the south of dreams; the one celebrated action, the other feeling; the one cultivated epic, the other lyric. There is no sharp geographical division possible in literature, of course; the heroes of the 'Song of Roland,' as of the other *chansons de geste*, came from all over the country, but their spirit is essentially Germanic. Lyric poets sang in the north, but the makers of Provence showed them the secrets of their art. The Arthurian romances represent the union of these two elements, forming a more national product, in one sense, than the *chansons de geste*, since, in mirroring the system of chivalry, they represent more truly the contribution of the whole country; a far less national product in another sense, since they deal largely with foreign material which makes no appeal to French patriotism.

It hardly need be said that the most striking change introduced by Provence into the literature of the age concerns the position of woman. We have noted that in stories of the Heroic Age love is generally, though not always, treated as secondary in interest to warlike adventure. The power of love was not ignored in the earlier period, but it was frequently made the motivation for more absorbing tales of combat, rather than celebrated for its own sake. A queen is chosen from a foreign people, war arises between her native and her adopted country, and the tragic alternative is presented her of choosing between her husband and children, and her father and brothers. Or a bride is gained without the consent of her father, who pursues and fights the abductor, while the distracted maiden is again torn by the claims of love and duty. Such are the typical motives of earlier story. Woman is a comrade if not an inferior, the object of animal passion or of manly love, but she is seldom sentimentalized over, and frequently quite forgotten. Heroes do not spend their time sighing for a lady; they carry her off, or find another, if they think one necessary to their happiness. Chivalry tolerates nothing like this; it raises woman to a new eminence, and makes her an altogether superior being, to be artificially wooed and won; and it replaces normal love by conventional and even immoral sexual relations. The chivalric hero weeps and wails, he loses his appetite, and sometimes his reason. Or he may pine in solitude, or perhaps quiet the throbbing of his wounded heart by impossible adventures in foreign lands. Frequently he takes to his bed, and refuses all comfort. The hero of Chaucer's 'Franklin's Tale' is a flower of chivalry; he

falls in love with a married woman (the fashionable
thing to do); she repulses him, and then

> In langour and in torment furious
> Two yeer and more lay wrecche Aurelius,
> Er any foot he mighte on erthe goon.

But for all such sickness there was always a cure, —
a single favoring glance from the bright eyes of the
lady !

The distinctive contribution of Provence to the romantic literature of the day is well illustrated by the
charming story of Aucassin and Nicolete.   It is hardly
representative of a class, for no other tale told with the
same peculiar blending of prose and verse has been preserved from this period, whatever may once have existed,
and in delicacy of conception and execution it is far
above the medieval average.   Nor is it in any way connected with King Arthur.   It is almost too familiar to
bear quotation, especially since Andrew Lang has made
it familiar to many who cannot read it in the original;
yet hardly anything else serves so perfectly as an illustration of the Provençal spirit, or bears repetition so
well.   It was probably written only some sixty or sev-
enty years later than the 'Song of Roland' in its present form, but a very few lines will show the striking
changes in contemporary social ideals which it reflects.

The description of the hero might stand well enough
for one of Charlemagne's knights.

Aucassin was the name of the damoiseau; fair was he, goodly,
and great, and featly fashioned of his body and limbs.   His hair
was yellow, in little curls, his eyes blue and laughing, his face
beautiful and shapely, his nose high and well-set, and so richly
seen was he in all things good that in him was none evil at all.

But the resemblance soon ends; he loves a pagan
maiden, captive among the Christians, and not at all
as the heroes of the *chansons de geste* loved a sultan's
daughter on occasion.

But so suddenly was he overtaken of Love, who is a great master,
that he would not, of his will, be dubbed a knight, nor take arms,
nor follow tourneys, nor do whatsoever him beseemed. Therefore
his father and mother said to him: " Son, go take thine arms, mount
thy horse, and hold thy land, and keep thy men, for if they see
thee among them more stoutly will they keep in battle their lives,
and lands, and thine, and mine." " Father," said Aucassin, " I
marvel that you will be speaking. Never may God give me aught
of my desire if I be made knight, or mount my horse, or face
stour and battle wherein knights smite and are smitten again, unless thou give me Nicolete, my true love, that I love so well."

Imagine Roland's answer if asked to choose between
Paradise and the fair Aude, and then listen to Aucassin,
when warned that a love like his will bar to him the en-
trance to Heaven.   "In Paradise what have I to win?
Therein I seek not to enter, but only to have Nicolete,
my sweet lady that I love so well."

The story is exceptional for its unaffected delicacy and
straightforwardness, but not for the prominence which it
gives to the element of love.   From the time of the Conquest until the Renaissance and even later, this was the
controlling interest of narrative poetry.   The golden
thread which guides one through the complicated mazes
of many a romance is likely to be provided by some
medieval Ariadne, waiting at the end of the skein for
the return of her champion.   Their love is often spontaneous in feeling and genuine in expression; the tales
of Erec and Enid, and of Tristram and Iseult, are full of
sincere and mutual devotion.   Iseult is no less straight-

forward than Brunhild. The curious artificiality in
matters of the heart which we have noted is particularly
characteristic of the more developed chivalric system;
when lovers are more concerned with rules of conduct
than with passion they naturally fail to act spontaneously.
The singular idea that woman should be a passive idol, a
mutely aloof creature playing with the tortured feelings
of the hero, and finally yielding through pity rather
than through passion, reaches its climax about a hundred years after 'Aucassin and Nicolete.' The 'Romance of the Rose' illustrates this well enough; the lady,
the Rosebud in the garden of Mirth, has nothing to do
throughout the thousands of lines in the poem, while
the lover is assailed by all conceivable emotions, and
reaches his goal at last only through long tribulation.
Yet this tendency is foreshadowed even in the words
with which Aucassin replies to the protestations of
Nicolete.

"Ah, fair sweet friend," said Aucassin, "it may not be that thou
shouldst love me even as I love thee. Woman may not love man
as man loves woman, for a woman's love lies in the glance of her
eye, and the bud of her breast, and her foot's tip-toe, but the love of
man is in his heart planted, whence it can never issue forth and pass
away."

The medieval knight had well-known duties towards
woman in general as well as towards the bright particular star whom he had chosen to serve. It was proper
for him to be tormented by love in the abstract if no appropriate object had presented herself for his devotion,
or to assist any lady who claimed his protection. The
ideal hero was the champion of all distressed ladies in a
world of oppression, and the court of Arthur was a

refuge for all such damsels.   Often, in the romances, some beautiful and unfortunate heroine interrupts the great king, while he and his knights are sitting at meat, by advancing boldly into the hall, attended by other ladies or by an ugly dwarf, and begging a boon of him.   Or a hero, riding through a leafy forest, meets a lady whom he has never seen before, and at her request abandons his business, turns about to escort her on her way, kills a giant and leaves him in his blood, or overcomes a champion hostile to her.   This comes close to our modern conception of the word "chivalry," — with a little exaggeration.   But the Middle Ages extended this to man's relations with his fellow-men, as well as with women.   "Courtoisie" meant much more than "courtesy" does to us.   Complete self-forgetfulness in the desire to be of assistance to others was as much a part of it as external fine manners.   All knights under affliction, oppressed by those more powerful than themselves, or laboring under magic spells, could look to the Round Table for redress.   Gawain rather than Arthur was the most perfect example of knightly generosity. With him, indeed, it becomes a kind of *desmesure*, or heroic recklessness.   He marries a loathly lady out of hand to help Arthur out of a tight place; he cuts off the head of his host on request without the slightest hesitation, — not because he realizes that this will free his afflicted entertainer from a spell, but because the perfect guest ought to do as he is told.   He pledges himself unhesitatingly to the most fantastic adventures when his aid has been invoked.   Common-sense is the last thing to deter him.

Such absurdities in the romances arise partly from

the peculiar character of the incidents typical of Celtic story. These imaginative elaborations, not the slight historical foundations, constitute the really important Celtic elements in the Arthurian legends. Celtic magic and mystery is of a peculiar sort, easier to distinguish from that of other countries by feeling than by definition. In Germanic stories, when supernatural beings appear, the wind still blows stiffly off the rocky headlands, and the keen sea-air strikes sharply in the face. Such beings are more gruesome because they are revealed in a world of everyday things. The roaring of Fafnir sounds from the sunlit forest, Hilde wakes the dead warriors in the chill clear northern night, and the Rhine daughters need no extraordinary conditions in order to appear bodily before Hagen and the Burgundians. The vivid description of the haunted pool in 'Beowulf' is exceptional; we may remember that there are those who think that Celtic elements have gone to the making of the tale. In the Arthurian stories, however, we have the sensation of moving in a world where natural phenomena are not only suspended, but not to be expected; the whole has something of the unreality of a dream. Merlin is only one magician in a world of enchanters and enchantment, and his illusions lose a little of their effect in the frequency of other-world mistresses, elfin knights, bespelled ladies, bewitched castles, and the like. Adventures have the inconsequence of dreams; a hideous Turk changes to a knight when his head is cut off; a serpent kisses Libeaus Desconus and becomes a beautiful woman; water is cast from a fountain upon a magic stone, and a storm arises in the enchanted wood, the birds cease to sing,

and a champion, armed to the teeth, plunges forward
ready for battle.   It is the logic of fairyland.

Matthew Arnold, in seeking to discover the distin-
guishing qualities of Celtic literature, quoted with
approval Henri Martin's phrase, "sentimental, always
ready to act against the despotism of fact." This
would be an almost equally happy characterization of
the Arthurian romances, with their lack of realism and
abundance of fantasy, their glorification of woman and
their insistence on the sensuous side of life. Arnold
furthermore suggested, though cautiously, the connection between the system of chivalry and the sentimentality of the Celtic temperament. "No doubt the sensibility of the Celtic nature, its nervous exaltation, have
something feminine in them, and the Celt is thus peculiarly disposed to feel the spell of the feminine idiosyn-
crasy; he has an affinity to it; he is not far from its
secret." Moreover, Arnold recognized that the exaggerations of medieval romantic poetry are such as
would naturally arise from characteristics like these.
"There is, in truth, a Celtic air about the extravagance
of chivalry, its reaction against the despotism of fact,
its straining human nature further than it will stand."
Yet while much of the absurdity as well as much of the
charm of medieval romance arises from the influence
which this people has exerted upon it, we may be sure
that, apart from the supernatural, it reflects to a large
degree the actual habits of thought of those among
whom it reached its fullest development, that it is characteristic of the spirit of the aristocracy of Western
Europe. We may see apt illustrations of this by com-
paring the Grail romances with memoirs of the Cru-

saders, in both of which appear the same exaltation, the same forgetfulness of fact in the demands of the ideal. Religion, to be sure, produces such exaltation in the highest degree, but religion and knightly behavior were so closely intertwined in the Middle Ages that separation of them is difficult. Chivalry was not only a rule of conduct for man in his relations with men and women, but equally so in his relations with God. It is not to be explained by any simple formula; it was a complicated growth, in the making of which many elements had their share. Its exaggerations and extravagances are thoroughly characteristic of the medieval temper, which was never content with halfway measures. We see the reflection of such absurdities in the plots of Shakspere's plays, the 'Merchant of Venice,' for example, in which Antonio's quixotic devotion to the interests of his friend is only paralleled by Portia's ludicrous method of selecting a husband. So Gawain, the model of courtesy, must sacrifice everything in order to satisfy the medieval ideal of the perfect gentleman.

There is, after all, a pathetic nobility about the very extravagances of chivalry. They reveal a people determined to pursue, regardless of consequences, a course of action which they believe to be right. Incongruity never disturbs them. Sir Gawain's adventures with the Green Knight, one of the most beautiful of all the Arthurian stories, are really no less absurd than much that befalls Don Quixote, and many of the causes which the average knight-errant espoused were really no more practical than tilting at windmills. But the underlying motive redeemed the action, just as Cervantes' caricature of chivalry was so far altered by the idealism of the hero that Don Quixote has stood for succeeding ages not alone as an embodiment of the grotesque features of knighthood, but of its tenderness and its devotion and its enthusiasm. We smile at Dulcinea del Toboso, but not at the spirit which makes fidelity to her a reason for championing the cause of all distressed ladies. The medieval love-conventions, artificial as they were, brought a new respect for women and a new gentleness into the heroic ideal. If chivalry did tend to become oversubtle and extravagant, it exercised a refining influence upon character which was sorely needed, and marked a great advance over the lack of the softer emotions in a Beowulf or a Roland.

It was impossible, too, that a system of conduct, guided and controlled by Christianity, which proclaims the brotherhood of man, and commands consideration for the poor and unfortunate, should not have had its effect upon the relations between the upper and the lower classes of society. St. Louis, denying magnificence to his household in order to give to the poor, was no isolated figure. His sacrifices may be explained as piety rather than as the generosity which springs from a larger social consciousness, perhaps, but similar tendencies manifest themselves in the life and literature of the time quite apart from religious motives. We have seen how little religion means to Aucassin, who prefers human love to the salvation of his soul, yet he gives money to help a poor and repulsive peasant whom he meets in the forest. The man has met with sore misfortune : —

"I was hireling to a rich villein, and drove his plough; four oxen had he. But three days since came on me a great misfortune, whereby I lost the best of mine oxen, Roger, the best of my team. Him go I seeking, and have neither eaten nor drunken these three days, nor may I go to the town, lest they cast me into prison, seeing that I have not wherewithal to pay. Out of all the wealth of the world have I no more than ye see on my body. A poor mother bare me, that had no more but one wretched bed; this have they taken from under her, and she lies in the very straw."

Aucassin gives him enough to replace the lost ox, and sends him on his way with new hope in his heart.

The consideration sometimes shown by the knights of Arthur to their inferiors is illustrated by an episode in the 'Morte Darthur' of Malory, which relates how Perceval, being in sore need of a horse, meets a yeoman in the forest, riding upon a hackney, and leading by the bridle a magnificent steed. Perceval begs of him the loan of the horse, but the yeoman refuses, realizing, however, that he is powerless to resist if the knight chooses to use force.

"Sir," said the yeoman, "I am right heavy for you, for a good horse would beseem you well, but I dare not deliver you this horse, but if ye would take him from me." "That will I not do," said Sir Percevale. And so they departed, and Sir Percevale sat him down under a tree, and made sorrow out of measure.

Mark Twain's description of the later Middle Ages, then, is only partly true, because he neglected the finer issues, and emphasized the more brutal features. He relieved the gloom of his picture by glimpses of brilliant pageantry, but he forgot that the truer contrast would have been the ideality of the times, and that in delicacy of feeling, in reverence for women, in courtesy to friend and foe, the Arthurian story foreshadowed much that is gentlest and best in modern civilization. Its sentiment sometimes became sentimentality, but the rudeness of the age required an excess of romance, just as the age of Richardson, tired of the classical insistence on the superiority of the head over the heart, welcomed the lachrymosities of Clarissa Harlowe. It is a pity to make King Arthur, the incarnation of the ideals of chivalry, responsible for the worst features of medieval society. Tennyson utilized the love of Tristram and Iseult to point a mid-Victorian moral, warping the plot and lowering the tone of the story to suit his purpose. It was a blunder; medieval romance ought not to be butchered to make a modern holiday. Tennyson was, on the whole, just to King Arthur, however; he represented him, as modern poets generally have done, as a champion of the forces of righteousness. This is the true Arthurian tradition, and has been for many centuries since the Celts first longed for the great hero's return from Avalon. It is, indeed, familiar enough to us to-day. A recent bit of magazine verse, pleading for social reform in America, voices the ideals which he symbolizes as triumphantly as do the romances of the Middle Ages.

> King Arthur's men have come again.
> They challenge everywhere
> The foes of Christ's Eternal Church.
> Her incense crowns the air.
> The heathen knighthood cower and curse
> To hear the bugles ring,
> But spears are set, the charge is on,
> Wise Arthur shall be king!

V

THE LEGEND OF THE HOLY GRAIL

"Comrades in arms! Mates of the Table Round!
Fair Sirs, my fellows in the bannered ring,
Ours is a lofty tryst! this day we meet,
Not under shield, with scarf and knightly gage,
To quench our thirst of love in ladies' eyes:
We shall not mount to-day that goodly throne,
The conscious steed, with thunder in his loins,
To launch along the field the arrowy spear :
Nay, but a holier theme, a mightier Quest —
'Ho! for the Sangraal, vanish'd Vase of God!'"

— HAWKER, ' Quest of the Sangraal.'

V

THE LEGEND OF THE HOLY GRAIL

ONE of the most interesting religious movements of the nineteenth century was the foundation and development of the Salvation Army. From small beginnings, from a mere handful of followers, it has become, at the present day, one of the chief influences for good in our great cities. There is scarcely a place of importance in the United States or in the British Empire where its music may not sometimes be heard in the streets at night, and where its exhortations to forsake sin and follow after righteousness are not helping hundreds who might otherwise feel themselves outcasts from the Kingdom of God. Every year the ranks of the Army are swelled with enthusiastic recruits. Substantial support has come to its work not only from the poor and unfortunate, but also from those who have the advantages of wealth and prosperity. If we think of it as one great organization, like the Roman Catholic Church or the Protestant Episcopal communion, we may safely reckon it as one of the most important religious bodies of modern times.

What has been the secret of its success? First, no doubt, the practical character of its teaching and of its religious activity. The sinner is brought face to face with the fundamental truths which all Christians

115

accept, but he is questioned little about theological details. He is given the right hand of fellowship, but he is bothered little with creeds. Moreover, he is helped in immediate and practical ways. If he is hungry, he is fed; if he is naked, he is clothed; if he is cold and homeless, he gets a warm place to sleep. The leaders of the movement were quick to recognize that you cannot save the soul of a man in physical distress. But there is yet another element which has done much to insure the success of the Salvation Army, — the imaginative appeal of its militant conception of Christianity. It is a body of soldiers, fighting the battles of Christ and His Church. This spirit of comradeship, of common interest in a cause which all have at heart, is expressed in the outward and visible form of military organization. Music and marching and ordered ranks and discipline appeal to the understanding of the simplest, and to the emotions of the most callous and the most degraded. Who can hear a military band pass by, with its stirring music of brass and cymbals, and the sharp rattle of its drums, without feeling a quickening of the pulse? Add to this the emotion of religious exaltation, and you have one great secret of the success of the Salvation Army. It is the incarnation, in practical form, of the spirit of the familiar hymn : —

> The Son of God goes forth to war,
>   A kingly crown to gain,
> His blood-red banner streams afar —
>   Who follows in His train?

By keeping the Salvation Army in mind we can understand something of the tremendous appeal of the great religious upheavals of the Middle Ages known as the

Crusades.   Beginning in the eleventh century, many
mighty armies were gathered together to fight the
battles of Christ; and enthusiasm to join these armies
and to take a personal part in these battles swept like
wildfire over Europe.   The contest was partly symbolical and spiritual, as in modern times, but it was
also a very real struggle with deadly weapons against
a valiant foe; and it had a definite concrete object.
The holy city of Jerusalem was in the hands of infidels,
who exalted the Crescent and trampled upon the Cross.
Shocking stories — doubtless often exaggerated — of
the ill-treatment of pilgrims and of the profanation of
holy places in the East added fuel to the flames of re-
sentment.   The duty of pious Christians was felt to be
to deliver the sacred city from its heathen masters.
To a people whose chief interest was war, and before
whom the fear of death and of the pains of hell was
constantly present, what could be more alluring than
a contest the mere participation in which would insure
forgiveness of sin and the prospect of salvation?   The
pomp and ceremony of armed expeditions, the waving
banners, the glittering armor, the serried ranks of enthusiastic volunteers, must have made a profound
appeal, particularly when the banner of the Cross was
unfurled, and men felt that minor quarrels were to be
forgotten in the defense of the Kingdom of God upon
earth.   All ranks of society allied themselves with the
Crusading armies.   It was no aristocrat's pilgrimage
merely; the poor and humble had their share.   Even
the children caught the general enthusiasm, and in a
pathetically ineffective imitation of the expeditions of
their elders, actually started for the beleaguered city

of the East. Landed possessions were forsaken, fortunes of private individuals were poured into the general treasury, the ties of home and family were broken.
One old Crusader, Jean de Joinville, says of his departure from his home, "And never would I turn my eyes
towards Joinville for fear my heart should melt within
me at thought of the fair castle I was leaving behind,
and my two children." If anything were needed to
exhibit the lofty idealism of the Middle Ages, the Crusades, although sometimes smirched with baser motives,
would furnish it. As Bishop Stubbs says, "They were
the first great effort of medieval life to go beyond the
pursuit of selfish and isolated ambitions; they were the
trial-feat of the young world, essaying to use, to the
glory of God and the benefit of mankind, the arms of
its new knighthood."

The story of these expeditions, which set out with such
high hopes and such pomp and pageantry, is pitiful, —
a tale of the ravages of disease, of slaughter and famine,
of treachery and cruelty, and of complete failure in the
great object at which they aimed. Into the details of this
story it is not necessary that we should go. The city of
Jerusalem was indeed captured by the Christians, some
thirty years after William of Normandy came to the
English shores, and a wise and noble man, Godfrey of
Bouillon, was placed on the throne of the newly created
kingdom of Jerusalem. But it was a tottering kingdom, at best, and less than a century later the holy city
fell into the hands of the Saracens. The later expeditions to regain it never achieved the measure of success
which the earlier one had attained; ambitions for conquest, for worldly dominion, and the petty rivalries of

those who should have stood shoulder to shoulder darken the glory of the later Crusades.   Moreover, they cost a fearful price in blood and suffering.   But unsuccessful, fantastic, and unpractical as the whole movement was, there was nevertheless something very fine even in its Quixotic idealism, in the willingness of men to expose themselves, for the sake of a great religious ideal, to every hazard of fortune which life can hold.

A prominent part in the Crusades, almost from the beginning, was taken by the Knights Templars, the great military and religious order founded for the defense of the Holy Sepulchre in Jerusalem, during the occupation of the city by the Christian kings.   Its members were bound by strict vows of poverty and chastity, and subjected to religious observances almost monastic in character.   Their chief duty was to strike down the enemies of the Church, never paying ransom nor asking for mercy.   Valiant fighters they were, riding with fanatical courage into the ranks of the Saracens, risking everything in a cause which they knew to be holy. Their attack on Ascalon was characteristic ; they forced their way into the heart of the city, with their foes on every hand, fighting desperately, until they were finally overcome by superior numbers, and slain in cold blood. Their courage was equaled by their simplicity, — at least in the earlier years of the order.   They shunned elaborate ornamentation on their horses and armor, and were distinguished by their mantles of pure white, typical of the stainlessness of their lives.   Upon these white mantles they later placed a red cross, in token of the holy cause which they had espoused.   By these insignia they are best known, and the Red Cross

has ever since stood as a symbol of chivalrous devotion
to the cause of Christianity. It is to-day the badge
of the great society which aims to relieve the sufferings
of the sick and wounded, but its true significance is
not always realized. Remembering the noble aims
and the self-sacrifice of the order of Knights Templars
in its earlier career, we may look with sympathy on its
misfortunes in the later evil days, when men grew en-
vious of its wealth and power, and crushed it with
calumniations. We prefer to think of its members as
St. Bernard described them: "All their trust is in the
Lord of Hosts, and in fighting for His cause they seek
a sure victory, or a Christian and an honorable death."

The devotion of the military life to the service of
God, exemplified in the Crusades and in the activities
of such organizations as the Templars, is expressed in
imaginative form in the legends of the Holy Grail. The
noblest aspirations of medieval chivalry are here set
forth symbolically. The story is not an offshoot
of the Crusades; its sources lie elsewhere, but it is another manifestation of the same idealism which made
the Crusades possible. It is vital partly because it
was a reflection of the age. In spite of great variation
of incident, it is, in general, marked by an elevation of
tone and a reverence of feeling which the romances too
often lack. Knightly prowess is here inspired by other
motives than the smiles of a lady; and the ambition
of the warrior to kill as many of his fellow-beings as
possible is tempered by the demands of religion and
humanity. Much that is fantastic makes its appearance in these stories; the characters often act in pro-
vokingly irrational ways, as if they had taken leave of

their common-sense. Knight-errantry here appears, at times, more absurd than ever. But this, too, was characteristic of the age; the enthusiasts who took the Cross generally had no clear idea of their precise plan of action; there was too little hard-headed business-like preparation about their expeditions. They were led on by a mighty impulse, and they left the practical side of their affairs to the guidance of chance, — or, as they would have expressed it, to the will of God. They did not believe that the Lord would most help those who help themselves, as Beowulf did; they believed that He would give strength to the Right, whether the Right had kept its powder dry or not. Hence much of the sickness and suffering, the famine and wandering, and in fact the ultimate failure of the Crusades. War cannot afford to be unbusinesslike, and the slaughter of thousands of Christians by Moslem swords must ultimately have convinced even the most dreamy enthusiast that God will not always give the victory to His chosen people. But if poets often conceived their allegories no more clearly than warriors did their plans of campaign, and if the result, in literature in life, was a certain vagueness and ineffectiveness, the fault is not so serious in poetry. The effect of a highly imaginative story may be heightened by mystic unreality. And a poet of romance can slay a thousand heathen by the prowess of a single hero, denying the pagans the consolation of any success whatsoever. We are not to look, then, in the legends of the Holy Grail for the more realistic side of chivalry, but rather for its more fantastic manifestations. But we are to remember that this very fantasy, which was in part a heritage from the Celtic treasure-house of magic and mystery, was also the expression of exaltation of feeling, of high striving for a noble ideal, which manifested itself in the Crusades.

What, then, is the story of the Holy Grail? The question is difficult to answer. Like other great medieval themes, it varies much in the hands of different story-tellers, both in details and in general conception. There is the usual wealth of episodes, following one another in bewildering succession. And these episodes are rearranged, in the different romances, with kaleidoscopic variety. Even among the principal incidents there is little consistency, there is no one story which can be called *the* legend of the Holy Grail. As time went on, one version was displaced by another, one hero was thrust aside to make way for a rival, the whole tone and import of the narrative changed. These alterations are interesting because they reflect corresponding changes in the ideal of the spiritual warrior, and they must be carefully considered. First, however, it is best to take one version as a point of departure, to observe the characteristics of one masterly telling of the tale in its earlier form, which may then be contrasted with another version reflecting the spirit of a later age.

The finest single conception of the story is that by the German poet, Wolfram von Eschenbach, one of the greatest of all medieval writers, who flourished about the time when Arthurian romance in Western Europe was at its high-water mark. It is also "on the whole the most coherent and complete version of the hero's career which we possess," and according to Alfred Nutt, one of the scholars who has best explained the growth of the legend, "the most interesting individual work of modern European literature prior to the 'Divina Commedia.'" There can hardly be a better choice for our purposes than this. Let us, then, in the beginning, follow the exploits of Parzival, or Percival, as we may call him for convenience in English, passing over details almost completely, and looking only at the more striking scenes, in order that the main outlines of the story as a whole may not be obscured.

Percival is brought up as a child by his mother in the depths of the forest, whither she has fled after his father's death. By secluding him from the world, and telling him nothing of the customs of knighthood, she hopes to keep him from the dangers which would otherwise beset him in his manhood. But one day he meets by chance a band of knights, clad in glittering armor, whom he takes for gods, so magnificent is their appearance. They tell him, if he would be a knight, to seek out the court of King Arthur, and enter his noble company. Reluctantly his mother lets him go, foreseeing that she will lose him forever. As he disappears in the distance, she falls dead, her heart broken at the loss of her son. But Percival rides on, until he comes to the court of King Arthur, where he is kindly received, in spite of the uncouthness of his appearance. His first exploit is the slaying of a mighty champion known as the Red Knight. Later he receives instruction in chivalric courtesy from a wise and friendly knight named Gurnemanz. He is cautioned to ask no questions, to restrain his curiosity. The true knight, he is told, should not be inquisitive.

After various exploits, he weds Queen Conduiramur,

but ere long he feels a desire to return to his mother, of whose death he knows nothing, and so he leaves his bride. As he rides forth, he comes to a lake, in the waters of which a richly dressed man is fishing. Percival begs of him a lodging for the night, and the fisherman invites him to be his guest. Arrived at the castle, the youth is hospitably received, and everything possible is done to make him comfortable. In the evening he is shown into a magnificent hall, lighted with many candles, and filled with a noble assemblage of knights. But the Fisher King, the lord of the castle, whom Percival had earlier seen on the lake, lies on a couch, suffering sorely from a grievous wound. He is wrapped in furs, and shivers before a great fire. Suddenly a wonderful thing happens; a squire comes into the hall carrying a lance, from the point of which there continually flow drops of blood. As he passes through the company, all break out in loud lamentations. After he has retired, a procession of damsels enters, one of whom bears aloft on a cushion the Holy Grail, a glittering stone, by means of which the whole company are miraculously fed. The Fisher King presents Percival with a costly sword. The youth desires to ask the meaning of the things that he has seen, but he remembers the instructions of his master, Gurnemanz, and is silent. On the following morning, when he awakes from a troubled sleep in the magnificent chamber which has been assigned to him, he is surprised to find the castle deserted. So he mounts his steed and rides away. As he leaves, the drawbridge is sharply closed behind him, and a voice reviles him for having failed to ask about the wonders which he saw in the castle. A little

farther on he meets a lady who tells him that he has
been in the castle of the Grail, and curses him for a
false knight because he has not asked about the trouble
of his host, and the mystery of the Grail and the Bleeding Lance.

After various adventures, Percival comes again to
the court of King Arthur, where he is received with all
honor. But suddenly the hideous woman Kondrie,
the messenger of the Grail, bursts into the hall, and
shames Percival before them all, since he had asked no
questions in the enchanted castle of Montsalvatch.

But weeping she gazed about her, and she cried as the tear-drops
  fell,
" Ah, woe unto thee! Montsalvatch, thou dwelling and goal of grief,
Since no man hath pity on thee, or bringeth thy woe relief."

For five years Percival seeks for the Castle of the
Grail, his soul full of revolt and despair. On Good
Friday he is rebuked by a pious knight for riding under
armor on the day of Christ's death, and sent to a hermit for confession. He tells the holy man that he is in
great trouble because he is parted from his wife, and
because he has failed to ask the question in the castle.
The hermit replies that they only find the Grail whom
God directs thither. He tells Percival more about the
Grail itself, — that it is a wonderful stone, upon which,
every Good Friday, a dove descending from Heaven
lays the consecrated Host. It is guarded by a body
of chosen knights, who must be of spotless purity
of life. Their King, the Fisher, had given himself up
to carnal love, and been wounded in consequence
by a poisoned spear. It has been his fate to suffer
agony until a hero comes to his castle, and asks

about his trouble. After receiving absolution, Percival returns to Arthur's court once more. The messenger Kondrie comes to him a second time, telling him that he is to be the new Keeper of the Grail. He goes to the castle, asks the question, heals the Fisher King, and becomes guardian of the Grail. He is restored to his wife, and his son is Lohengrin, Knight of the Swan.

All this is truly as irrational and fantastic as a fairy-tale. This Fisher King, suffering from a wound which can be healed only by the asking of a question, this spear continually dripping blood, this stone which feeds a whole company of people, this strange castle, filled at night with feasting and revelry, with brave knights and busy servants, and in the morning silent and deserted save for a spectral voice ringing out over the battlements, — all these things are the stuff that dreams are made of. They accord ill with such a religious feature as the descent of the dove, the symbol of the Holy Ghost; and the sanctity of the consecrated Host seems hardly in keeping with the practical working of an automatic food-provider, such as the Grail seems to be. How strange, too, is the verdict of the tale on the hero's action! He is constantly blamed for having failed to ask the question, but his fault seems slight, — it may even be called a virtue, since it springs in the beginning from his desire to pay due heed to the demands of courtesy. How are all these incongruities and fantastic motives to be explained?

The story was, in all probability, originally purely pagan, wholly unconnected with Christian symbolism. If we could get back to its beginnings, we should discover that it has grown, to a large extent, out of the weird imagination of the Celts. They were fond of marvelous adventures, which could be performed only by fantastic devices. So this has perhaps developed from tales in which a young hero penetrated into a castle and freed a kinsman from enchantment by asking a magic question, or got possession of a wonder-working symbol of plenty, which, when rightly used, would bring prosperity to all those about it. The Grail was once, in all likelihood, a pagan talisman of plenty, and not a holy cup at all. In Celtic stories there are all sorts of ways to break the spells which fetter beings who have been bewitched — sometimes highly fantastic ways, like decapitation. The head of a hideous dwarf is cut off, and he stands forth in his own shape as a brave knight. Gawain, we remember, married a loathly lady, and agreed to let her have the say in their family affairs, whereupon the spell was broken, and she was transformed into a woman of surpassing beauty. A kiss has equal potency in dispelling the effects of magic. In a region where things happen as strangely as this, there is no reason why the asking of the proper question should not heal a sick man, or break the spell lying on an enchanted palace. Sometimes questioning is the reverse of judicious; in the story of Lohengrin the lady loses her supernatural husband because she asks him whence he came in the beginning. Fairyland is a most illogical place, as we have seen, — or rather it is a place with a queer logic of its own, like the wonderful country the little girl found on the other side of the looking-glass.

It is possible that the Grail story is to be traced ultimately to ritualistic observances in honor of a god of fertility or vegetation. In certain versions of the tale, the asking of the magic question causes the country to burst into bloom, and the inhabitants bless the hero for having freed them from the curse of barren fields and sterile trees. The wounded king may then have been originally the god of fertility himself, Adonis or Tammuz, or his hierophant, and the youthful knight who visits the castle an initiate into the secret and symbolic rites of nature-worship. If this be the case, these rites, which bore analogies to the communion instituted in memory of the Last Supper of Christ, must later have been brought into conformity with Christian observances, and the originally pagan character of the ceremonial completely forgotten. There would appear to be particularly clear evidences of this nature-cult in the adventures of Gawain at the Grail Castle, as told by one of the continuators of Chrétien's 'Perceval.' Gawain partly succeeds in breaking the spell which lies upon castle and land, but not completely. Discussion of this matter must rest very largely upon conjecture; no satisfactory proof of the "nature-ritual theory" is likely to be forthcoming. It is highly probable, however, that Gawain was the first of the knights of Arthur to figure as the Grail hero, that even Percival was only later made the chosen champion. The character of Gawain, like that of other Arthurian heroes, degenerated in later days, until he appears in Malory and Tennyson as anything but the ideal knight. But in the earlier romances he is the incarnation of perfect chivalry.

A later age rationalizes the absurdities in these tales, and turns them to account for its own ends. The wound

of the Fisher King was probably originally due to his
misfortune, not his fault, but the story which has just
been outlined makes it a punishment for broken vows,
for fighting in the cause of unlawful love. Similarly,
the failure of the youth to ask the question is attributed
by Wolfram von Eschenbach to lack of human sympathy. In later years, after Percival has had experience with the sorrows which life brings, he can truly
feel for the wounded monarch in his agony of pain, and
heal him by the force of human compassion. Thus a
master-poet has softened and refined the cruder motives
of the old story, and made it point a profound moral
lesson. Time brings these transformations to popular
story, as it relieves the harsh outlines of ancient castles,
overlaying them with verdure, and giving them a fresher
and more delicate charm.

More important than the interpretation of the absurdities of the story in terms of the development of
human character is the Christian symbolism. The
sacred object, the Grail, is guarded by those divinely
chosen for such service, and is itself given miraculous
power by the direct interposition of the Holy Ghost.
The later the story, the more the religious element is
emphasized. That the Grail had been a pagan talisman
of plenty was forgotten, and it was identified as the
cup in which the blood of Christ was caught after the
Crucifixion, or with a vessel used by him at the Last
Supper. Poets took delight in elaborating the early
history of the sacred chalice, before it was finally de-
posited in the Grail Castle, and in developing a mass of
legend as detailed, but not as interesting, as the story of
its achievement by the destined knight.

> The cup, the cup itself, from which our Lord
> Drank at the last sad supper with his own.
> This, from the blessed land of Aromat —
> After the day of darkness, when the dead
> Went wandering o'er Moriah — the good saint
> Arimathæan Joseph, journeying brought
> To Glastonbury, where the winter thorn
> Blossoms at Christmas, mindful of our Lord.
> And there awhile it bode; and if a man
> Could touch or see it, he was heal'd at once
> By faith, of all his ills.   But then the times
> Grew to such evil that the holy cup
> Was caught away to heaven, and disappear'd.

The symbol of the holy chalice thus came to stand for
the religious aspirations of the Knights of the Round
Table, and the achievement of the Grail for the triumph
of a life of purity and of devotion to high ideals.   This
religious element, then, brought with it an entire change
in the conception of the story.   What had in the beginning been won by valor, was now unattainable without
virtue.   What was originally a quest for revenge, or
for the breaking of enchantment, or for the acquisition
of wonder-working objects, now became a supreme effort
to attain a sacred relic by means of which man might be
brought face to face with manifestations of Divine
power on earth.

Strangely enough, this insistence on the religious
element in the story ultimately weakened its vigor, and
injured its artistic completeness.   The chief stress was
laid in the later versions on the absolute holiness of the
knight who was to achieve the Grail.   He became a
saint, but he ceased to be a normal man.   In the story
which we have just considered, the successful outcome

of the undertaking depended, as we have seen, upon the gaining of human sympathy. The reason why Percival became keeper of the Grail at the end was because he had progressed, through misfortune and varied experience of life, to such a compassionate understanding of human suffering that he could truly ask the Fisher King about his trouble without being moved by mere curiosity. This is an ethical rather than a religious conception, and yet we should all agree that a religious experience which brought such a result was well worth while. But such a view of the duty of a man towards his fellowmen did not satisfy the sterner spirits of the Middle Ages, into whose hands the story of the Grail ultimately passed. To them religion did not mean the use of all the faculties of man in a sensible and normal way; it meant the total suppression of all instincts which might be turned to baser ends. The truly holy man was conceived to be the one who lived for religion alone, and shut all other thoughts out of his heart. The love of wife and child all the beauty and romance of life, was to be disregarded, and religious exaltation was to take their place. Sympathy with the present sufferings of mankind was to be subordinated to sympathy with the agonies of Christ on the Cross. This ascetic conception of life, which came partly as a reaction against laxity in religious matters, affected profoundly the great symbolical story of the Grail Knight. His whole character came to be differently imagined. Great stress had always been laid on his purity, ever since the time when the Grail had been conceived as a holy object, but this quality was now insisted upon in the narrowest way. The hero became a sort of recluse in armor, fighting his way through a sinful world, to the demands of which he paid little heed, but keeping always before him a glorious vision, — Christ's blood streaming in the firmament in the chalice of the Grail.   To this perfection Percival could not attain, — his achievements were too worldly in men's eyes; and so a new figure was created, the "maiden knight" Galahad.

Tennyson has summed up the character of this hero in one of the most striking and beautiful of his early poems.   With the ecstasy of the mystic and the single-heartedness of the fanatic, Galahad presses through battle hearing only the sound of hymns; he sees homes and hearthstones about him, but he rides ever madly on to the goal.

> When on my goodly charger borne
>   Thro' dreaming towns I go,
> The cock crows ere the Christmas morn,
>   The streets are dumb with snow.
> The tempest crackles on the leads,
>   And, ringing, springs from brand and mail;
> But o'er the dark a glory spreads,
>   And gilds the driving hail.
> I leave the plain, I climb the height;
>   No branchy thicket shelter yields;
> But blessed forms in whistling storms
>   Fly o'er waste fens and windy fields.
>
> *   *   *   *   *   *
>
> The clouds are broken in the sky,
>   And thro' the mountain-walls
> A rolling organ-harmony
>   Swells up and shakes and falls.
> Then move the trees, the copses nod,
>   Wings flutter, voices hover clear:

'O just and faithful knight of God.
    Ride on! the prize is near.'
So pass I hostel, hall, and grange;
    By bridge and ford, by park and pale,
All-arm'd I ride, whate'er betide,
    Until I find the Holy Grail.

This, then, is the spirit of the hero of the later versions of the story, of Galahad as contrasted to Percival, of the man of ascetic purity and narrow singleness of vision, rather than of the man who comes through knowledge of sin to a truer consciousness of his relations to his fellow-men.

This difference between the earlier and the later conceptions of the Grail Knight is well seen in his relations to women. The romances in general, as we have seen in the last lecture, were not what we should call moral; they often exalted illicit love. But their recognition of the part which woman ought to play in the life of man, even if it was sometimes fantastically conceived, according to the artificial code of chivalry, nevertheless represented an advance over the ideals of the age preceding. In the story of Percival, in the form which has just been outlined, the hero is married. In the excitements of the world, he neglected the duties which he owed to his wife, but, at the end, in his confession to the hermit, he felt the necessity of her love, and the part that wedlock ought to play in his life. The Fisher King was punished because, while under a vow to remain pure in heart, he had loved unlawfully. Percival was punished partly because he had treated with neglect his wife and the mother of his children. When he returns to her he is not less worthy to be the Keeper of the Grail because he is at her side, but more worthy. Galahad, on the other hand, is held more holy because he has never known the love of woman. He has never felt the touch of a maiden's hand within his own. For this reason he comes to be exalted above Percival, and especially above such knights as Gawain, the typical squire of dames, whose many love-adventures will not bear very close scrutiny, and as Launcelot, the unlawful lover of Queen Guinevere. These knights set out on the Quest, but they are not virtuous enough for the achievement of the Grail. Launcelot does indeed penetrate into the castle, but in the ecstasy of his vision he realizes his own unworthiness. In these later Grail stories, then, love is really made subordinate to asceticism, — a curious transformation for romance! It is easy to see how this might have come about, however, — even in the earlier form of the story the Templars, who guard the sacred chalice in the castle, are forbidden to marry, and great stress is laid on their personal purity. But there was no such rigid insistence on celibacy for the Keeper of the Grail; he was free to marry if he chose. Ultimately, on the other hand, the chosen knight gets to be a sexless abstraction, a bloodless incarnation of holiness. Medieval asceticism indeed laid its finger heavily on the highest romantic ideal of the age of chivalry. Instead of striving to correct the evils of the age by preaching a broad and tolerant view of love and marriage, it rushed to the opposite extreme, and sought to shrivel up all the beauty and holiness of the love of woman in the white fire of its religious ardor.

Modern versions of medieval legends sometimes give a wholly false idea of the attitude of the Church in the

Middle Ages towards earthly love. In Maeterlinck's poetic drama 'Sister Beatrice,' the Virgin Mother herself descends to earth and assumes the guise of the erring nun, who has left the convent for the love of Prince Bellidor. The other sisters do not know that any change has taken place. Long after, broken in body and spirit by the faithlessness of her lover and the cruelty of the world, Sister Beatrice creeps back to the convent once more, and discovers the miracle that has taken place in her absence. Because of the purity of her affection for Prince Bellidor, her sin and her desertion have been forgiven her. The point of the whole play is summed up in the Virgin's own words: —

> There is no sin that lives
> If love have vigil kept;
> There is no soul that dies,
> If love but once have wept.

But this is thoroughly foreign to the spirit of the medieval church, — no writer of those days, surely, would have attributed such words as these to the Virgin. It is interesting to compare with Maeterlinck's play its source, the Middle Dutch legend of Beatrice, written in the fourteenth century, which may be read in a graceful modern English translation.[1] In this version of the story, the Virgin takes the place of Beatrice, because the nun had always been faithful in her service. The miracle is here a reward for devotion to the Mother of God, not a sign that Heaven has pardoned an evil act through the purity of feeling which prompted it. In the Middle Ages, a nun unfaithful to her vows

[1] *Beatrice, a Legend of Our Lady*, translated by Harold De Wolf Fuller. (Cambridge, 1909.)

might be forgiven by the Church because of her love for the Virgin, but she would never have been forgiven because of her passion for an earthly lover, however pure such a passion might have been.

The earlier form of the Grail story, with Percival as the hero, which was told so exquisitely by the early German master Wolfram von Eschenbach, has been made familiar in modern times by the genius of Richard Wagner. His music-drama 'Parsifal' is deeply religious in tone, yet it brings out much the same ethical lesson as its prototype, — that true sympathy with suffering must come from bitter experience. There is much in Wagner's work which represents an advance over the version of eight centuries earlier, — a simpler and more coherent form, and a deeper spiritual significance. The German people may well be proud to have in their national literature two such lofty conceptions of the great theme of the Holy Grail. To the English-speaking peoples, on the other hand, the later version of the tale is better known. In his 'Idylls of the King,' as in the early poem which has just been quoted, Tennyson celebrated Galahad as the successful knight, but without essentially altering his character. William Morris, too, made Galahad put love out of his heart, and conquer in the end, after all others had failed, through religious devotion and purity of life. In the famous mural paintings in the Boston Public Library, Abbey has given the place of honor to the red-robed maiden knight, and he, too, has shown him leaving his bride, a pathetic little figure in her wreath of roses, for the greater blessedness of the search for the Grail. Deeply mystic is the beautiful 'Quest of the Sangraal' by Stephen Hawker, an

English clergyman who later became a Roman Catholic. In this, as perhaps might be expected, the ascetic note is again emphasized.

The prevalence of this general conception of the story in modern English poetry is largely due to the influence of Sir Thomas Malory. His 'Morte Darthur,' written over three centuries later than the great German version which has just been outlined, may well stand as presenting the later ideal of the Grail hero, an ideal developed, as we have seen, under monkish influences. Malory's story of the quest was not original; it was copied from a French romance in prose, in which some man of lofty but narrow religious views had made the hero the incarnation of physical purity, the purity which comes from the repression of natural instincts. The Galahad that Sir Thomas puts before us is really not his own creation, then. He was a translator rather than a story-teller; his great contribution was in making the Arthurian stories accessible to his countrymen in picturesque and melodious English prose. He did not give his work any characteristically English coloring, nor did he attempt to set forth specifically English views. But he produced an English classic, which has become the great storehouse of Arthurian romance for those whose mother-tongue is English. It is thus partly due to accident that the ascetic conception of the Grail hero has become most familiar to English readers, and not because this conception was most in accord with the ideals of their forefathers. Had Malory happened to have before him an earlier form of the tale, matters might have been different. His whole rendering of the Arthurian story, however, is like an Indian summer of the age of chivalry. At the time of the Discovery of America, when his book was gaining its earliest popularity, the old feudal institutions were passing, and English literature was beginning to reflect the spirit of a newer age, the Renaissance. The 'Morte Darthur' is one of the last leaves on the tree of medieval romance, splendidly colored, it is true, but already withering, a mere relic of the glory of the vanished springtime.

The selfishness in the character of Galahad was apparently felt by Lowell to such a degree that he boldly departed from precedent and chose as the hero of his version of the Grail legend Sir Launfal, a minor figure of Arthurian romance. In this finely conceived poem, Lowell attacked the self-centered pride, the utter forgetfulness of others, which accompanies the deep religious ecstasy of the later Grail questers. In the vision which comes to Sir Launfal as he lies asleep, he sees himself flashing forth in his unscarred mail in the pride of his youth, bound on a holy mission, but with no real charity for the leper crouching at his gate. Then, in old age, having failed in his search for the sacred vessel, he comes, like Percival, to a true sympathy with the afflicted man, and he breaks with him his last crust of bread, and fills the cup for him at the icy stream. On a sudden, the leper stands up glorified, as Christ indeed, and in the words which he speaks to Launfal we know that the knight has at last been successful in his quest.

> " Lo, it is I, be not afraid !
> In many climes, without avail,
> Thou hast spent thy life for the Holy Grail;
> Behold, it is here, — this cup which thou
> Didst fill at the streamlet for me but now:

This crust is my body broken for thee,
This water His blood that died on the tree;
The Holy Supper is kept, indeed,
In whatso we share with another's need;
Not what we give, but what we share,
For the gift without the giver is bare;
Who gives himself with his alms feeds three, —
Himself, his hungering neighbor, and Me."

The medieval legends of the Holy Grail often represent, then, a short-sighted religious ideal, and a fantastic
and unpractical notion of its attainment. And yet,
in spite of all this, there is something very inspiring
about their sincerity and enthusiasm. We can forgive
the fanatic his blindness to larger issues, we can forgive the mystic his struggle for a perfection which is to
affect himself alone, in remembering their single-hearted
devotion to a lofty aim. It is better, surely, to have
a narrow or an unpractical religion, than to have no
religion at all, or a religion which is lukewarm and unconvinced. The Quest of the Holy Grail, even in its
narrower conception, may have a significance and a
message for our own age, which is often said to be lacking in true religious enthusiasm, which is often called
a day of doubt and questioning, a day of too little
simple faith and genuine emotion. We are so encompassed about on every hand by the interests of a strenuous existence, so dazzled by the marvels of an era which
has indeed snatched the thunderbolts from heaven and
the scepter from tyrants, that we may have lost something of the old wonder at the majesty of God in
wonder at the achievements of man. Would such a
sweeping religious exaltation as the Crusades be possible
to-day? We have tried to see an instance of a similar

enthusiasm in the growth of the Salvation Army, but
the parallel is far from perfect.   More of such enthusiasm
as animated the Crusaders we undoubtedly need nowadays.   Reckless and even narrow idealism is not always
a bad thing, — it is the ideal itself which counts.   However it may stand with us, the men of the Middle Ages
could hardly escape being touched to finer issues by
having such a theme as this before them.   Perhaps unconsciously, poets made the old pagan story into a reflection of their own times.   The quest of a knight for
the Holy Grail is only an allegory of the struggle of the
Crusader to reach, through difficulties and discourage-
ments as great as those raised by enchantment, the
Holy Sepulcher at Jerusalem.   In poetry, this lofty
theme partly supplanted baser subjects, just as the
heroism of the Crusades partly supplanted baser motives
in a time of violence and oppression.   In spite of irreverence and immorality and cynicism, the legend of the
Holy Grail stood to the end for the highest knightly
ideal.

In turning now to the story which gibes at religion
and scoffs at morality, the History of Reynard the Fox,
we must keep constantly before us the significance of
this ideal.   Its very exaggerations are necessary to
balance the extremes in the cynical story of Reynard.
In the Middle Ages, as we have seen, the golden mean
was seldom observed; religion and cynicism were alike
pushed to their limits.   The two stories of the Holy
Grail and of Reynard the Fox are as sharply contrasted
as the sculptured saint on a cathedral, gazing with vague,
fixed stare beyond a world of vanity to a heavenly goal,
and the gargoyle hard by, leering up in his face with

impish irreverence. Each represents a special manifestation of medieval social consciousness, and each
has contributed, the gargoyle as well as the saint, the
saint as well as the gargoyle, to the saner and better-
balanced life of modern times.

VI

THE HISTORY OF REYNARD THE FOX

But ye that holden this tale a folye,
As of a fox, or of a cok and hen,
Taketh the moralitee, good men.

— CHAUCER.

VI

THE HISTORY OF REYNARD THE FOX

In Maeterlinck's charming fantasy, 'The Blue Bird', there is a pretty scene in which the animals and the household objects in the cottage of a poor peasant are transformed into the semblance of human beings through the arts of the Fairy Berylune. The little boy, the hero of the play, turns a diamond button in a magic cap, and suddenly all sorts of wonders come to pass. The Water and the Milk become graceful undulating ladies, the Bread waddles about the stage in the shape of a fat, puffy man, the Fire, in human form, darts hither and thither with the agility of a dancer, and the Sugar makes soothing remarks, or breaks off the tips of his fingers as sweets for the children. In the adventures of the little boy and his sister the Dog and the Cat take particularly active parts, the one faithful and affectionate, the other sly and hypocritical. Their transformation is not, perhaps, so startling, for even as dumb animals they seem more human than the food and drink. Who has not been reminded of disagreeable people of his acquaintance by the ingratitude or selfishness of a favorite cat, or felt his heart warm to the truly human sympathy of a pet dog? So it is in the play; the children barely escape the machinations of Tylette the

145

cat, who, though once their playfellow, has no hesitation about betraying them, while to the very end Tylo
the dog is the embodiment of complete devotion.
These are the most real of all the actors in the little
story who are transformed by the fairy's magic, because
their natures and ours are separated by so slight a
barrier, which a touch of enchantment can easily break
down.

We almost forget, in the charm and originality with
which Maeterlinck has worked out this conception, that
it is really not new, but a part of a tradition as old as
story-telling itself.   There has hardly been an age since
the world began, as far back as we have any knowledge
of popular literature, when animals and inanimate things
have not spoken with the tongues of men, and acted like
human beings.   A Fairy Berylune has always been on
hand, — we may call her Imagination, if we choose —
to transform the beast-world for children of a larger
growth, as well as for those of tenderer years.   The
most familiar animal tales of the present day are only
in a small degree the creation of modern times.   Joel
Chandler Harris has made us acquainted with Brer Fox
and Brer Rabbit, but he learned it all from many an
Uncle Remus of the South, who inherited it ultimately
from ancestors in whose African forests animals talked
and acted like men.   Kipling narrates the adventures
of the boy Mowgli among the beasts and birds of the
Indian jungle, but in spite of many touches due to
Kipling's imagination, Mowgli might just as well have
lived three thousand years ago, when tales of half-
human animals were popular in India, as at the present
day.   Again, the very name "Æsop" attached to the

fables which the children read in the nursery is a survival of the tradition that they were composed in classical antiquity by a gifted slave. In short, whenever we
follow story-telling back to its sources, we are sure
to find anthropomorphic conceptions of animals and
things. Chaucer, in telling his story of the Cock and
the Fox, half apologizes : —

> For thilke tyme, as I have understonde,
> Bestes and briddes coude speke and singe.

But "thilke tyme" means all the ages past in which men
have loved good stories. And it has never passed;
we still endow animals with human attributes whenever
we give our fancy rein. So Maeterlinck, in his charming tale, has only added a drop to a sea of story-telling
which washes the farthest shores that exploration can
reach.

After its universality, the most distinctive quality
of this beast-literature is its popular character, in the
sense that it has always been, in its earlier stages,
the possession and the product of the people themselves.
Individual writers and poets may have reshaped it, but
it is not they who have made it vital and significant.
It is, in Jusserand's phrase, "an expression and outcome
of the popular mind." It is full of the lively imagination and the keen observation of those who are more
familiar with fields and forests than with pen and ink.
In the beginning it lives by word of mouth, told at the
fireside, after the day's work is over, or during the tedium
of winter evenings, — whenever, in short, a tale is in
order. Whether we find it on the banks of the Nile or
the Ganges, the Mississippi or the Rhine, it is curiously

constant in its essentials, — true to the peculiarities
of the people among whom it has developed, but also
true to the spirit of popular story.   Curious similarities
of incident appear, for which nobody has ever been able
to account in a really satisfactory way, and which are,
provided literary influence is out of the question, a
pretty sure indication of popular origin.   A tale in
Iceland may be essentially the same as one in New
Guinea; the South American Indians have a story about
the tortoise which is a good parallel to one told by
Uncle Remus about the terrapin.   Scholars have spent
much time and thought in trying to decide how all these
peoples can have evolved practically identical narratives
independently.   The fundamental likeness in the imaginative processes of primitive folk may account in
part for the presence of the same story in widely separated communities of a similar degree of intelligence
and culture, but it hardly makes the matter entirely
clear.   Of this particular kind of intellectual fellowship
we have but little in the twentieth century.   We have
substituted, it is true, a more desirable sort, but it is
odd to reflect that we might be in some respects closer
to foreign peoples if we were all in a state of savagery,
with no transatlantic cables or steamers, no books or
newspapers, than we are with all the bonds of intercourse
of modern civilization.

The simplicity and universality of these animal
stories may be illustrated by Uncle Remus's account
of how Brer Rabbit lost his long bushy tail.   It will be
observed that this story explains the reason why Brer
Rabbit and all his family have had short tails ever since.
The main part of the story is as follows : —

" One day Brer Rabbit wuz gwine down de road shakin' his long, bushy tail, w'en who should he strike up wid but ole Brer Fox gwine amblin' long wid er big string er fish !   W'en dey pass de time er day wid wunner nudder, Brer Rabbit, he open up de confab, he did, en he ax Brer Fox whar he git dat nice string er fish, en Brer Fox, he up 'n 'spon' dat he kotch um, en Brer Rabbit, he say whar'bouts, en Brer Fox, he say down at de babtizin' creek, en Brer Rabbit he ax how, kaze in dem days dey wuz monstus fon' er minners, en Brer Fox, he sat down on a log, he did, en he up'n tell Brer Rabbit dat all he gotter do fer ter git er big mess er minners is ter go ter de creek atter sun down, en drap his tail in de water en set dar twel daylight, en den draw up a whole armful er fishes, en dem w'at he don't want, he kin fling back.   Right dar's whar Brer Rabbit drap his water-million, kaze he tuck'n sot out dat night en went a fishin'.   De wedder wuz sorter cole, en Brer Rabbit, he got 'im a bottle er dram en put out fer de creek, en w'en he got dar he pick out a good place, en he sorter squot down, he did, en let his tail hang in de water.   He sot dar, en he sot dar, en he drunk his dram, en he think he gwine-ter freeze, but bimeby day come, en dar he wuz.   He make a pull, en he feel like he comin' in two, en he fetch nudder jerk, en lo en be-holes, whar wuz his tail ? "

"Did it come off, Uncle Remus ?" asked the little boy, presently.

"She did dat !" replied the old man with unction. "She did dat, and dat w'at make all deze yer bob-tail rabbits w'at you see hoppin en skaddlin' thoo de woods."

We can readily imagine how much a story like this would appeal to a popular audience. And this same incident is told, with variations, all over the world, — in Finland, in Scotland, in Hungary, in Greece, in Africa. In the Soudan, where ice is unknown, the central episode has to be something different : the tail is caught, not in the frozen pool, but in the tangle of roots and branches under the waters of a tropical swamp. The actors vary, too. In the commonest medieval French version it is the bear and not the rabbit that is

the victim.   But the main outlines are quite the same.
The fox is roasting eels, and the bear is attracted by
the savory odor.   The same trick is played, the bear
drops his tail — once long and bushy like the fox's —
into the chilly water, and is obliged to leave the end
of it sticking in the ice in order to escape the dogs and
huntsmen.   Consequently the bear has had a short tail
ever since.

This general type of story is of great antiquity as well
as of wide distribution over the globe.   It is not strange
that it has been popular, with its simple outline and its
dramatic ending.   But there is still another reason for
its perpetuation; it responds to the desire of the un-
developed mind for explanations of natural phenomena.
Primitive people and children are much alike; their
minds work in a similar way.   The insistent demand
of a child to be told the reason for anything which he
does not understand is familiar to all of us; these
stories, in the beginning, answered the "whys" of men
who were still as untrained and uneducated as children.
This perhaps explains why they have such an absorbing interest for the modern nursery.   But you may
see traces of them in the 'Jatakas,' or Buddhist Birth-
Stories, which arose long before the Christian era,
as well as in the 'Just-So Stories.'   In the latter,
Kipling, writing for his own children, has drawn from
the great storehouse of popular literature which he
knows so well.   "Why does the Leopard have such
funny spots?" asks the child.   The story tells the
reason: the Leopard had a good chance to have his
skin "done over," and the Ethiopian, who had just
changed his skin himself, volunteered to undertake the

job of marking him.   There is some debate about the design.

"Think of Giraffe," said the Ethiopian.   "Or if you prefer stripes think of Zebra.   They find their spots and stripes give them perfect satisfaction."

"Umm," said the Leopard.   "I wouldn't look like Zebra — not for ever so."

"Well, make up your mind," said the Ethiopian, "because I'd hate to go hunting without you, but I must if you insist on looking like a sun-flower against a tarred fence."

"I'll take spots, then," said the Leopard, "but don't make 'em too vulgar-big.   I wouldn't look like Giraffe — not for ever so."

"I'll make 'em with the tips of my fingers," said the Ethiopian. "There's plenty of black left on my skin still.   Stand over !"

Then the Ethiopian put his five fingers close together (there was plenty of black on his new skin still) and pressed them all over the Leopard, and wherever the five fingers touched they left five little black marks, all close together.   You can see them on any Leopard's skin you like, Best Beloved.   Sometimes the fingers slipped and the marks got a little blurred; but if you look closely at any Leopard now you will see that there are always five spots — off five fat black finger-tips."

But while animal tales are thoroughly popular and universal, and while their incidents may be very similar in different countries and at different times, they are none the less thoroughly characteristic of the people and the age to which they severally belong.   The stories of Uncle Remus, for all they may have their counterparts on the river Amazon or in the Middle Ages, represent, as their transcriber says, "the shrewd observation, the curious retorts, the homely thrusts, the quaint comments, and the human philosophy of the race of which Uncle Remus is the type."   In the same way, the medieval versions of these stories are perfect reflections

of the society which produced them.   We have already
seen how little the Middle Ages were troubled by lack
of originality in plot, how authors aimed to have it
thought that they were merely reproducing tradition,
but how impossible it was for them to retell a story
without giving it the distinctive stamp of their own
times.   They had no historical sense, they could not
depict the life of other countries or of other ages except
in terms of their own day and their own country.   Their
limitations were particularly evident, for instance, in
treating classical material.   They may have made the
tales of Greece and Rome quaint and curious, but they
also made them stiff and grotesque.   No amount of
medieval magnificence could make Alexander or Æneas
seem at his ease in the trappings of a feudal knight.
But such limitations did not hamper their treatment
of the animal stories.   There is no material so flexible,
so easily interpreted in terms of the present, and still
so natural and convincing.   Animals are always with
us, and their habits do not materially change.   Once
admit that they are to act like men, and their appearance in the garb of the present day seems entirely
suitable.

It is, indeed, almost impossible for the story-teller
not to interpret the characteristics of animals in terms
of his own age, if he makes them speak with human
voices, and reason like human beings.   He must de-
lineate them in the same way that he would his fellow-
men, and it is his fellow-men who must serve as models.
In setting forth the character of the Fox, he may very
likely have consciously in mind some persons with
whom he is acquainted, men of subtle shifts and crafty

schemes, and if he does not consciously think of such
people, he is likely unconsciously to have their images
in the back of his brain.   Moreover, his narrative will
be influenced by similarities between the intercourse of
beasts and the social life of men.   If he makes the animals hold a meeting, he may well model this assemblage
on some deliberative body with which he is familiar.
The peculiar manners and customs of the day are sure
to attach themselves to the world of animals, when
once these are anthropomorphically conceived.

Such a story-teller may even go further, and see in
certain species of animals the reflection of certain large
groups or classes of human society.   He knows that the
cat pursues the mouse, and that the hawk swoops down
upon the chickens, and if he lives in an age when the
weak are oppressed by the wealthy and influential
members of the community, he may well make the
hawk or the cat stand for the more rapacious types of
human beings.   Sympathy with the people and a keen
sense of the shortcomings of the ruling classes can hardly
fail to influence the telling of such animal tales, in which
pity for the weak is accompanied by a pleasant realiza-
tion of the faults and failings of their stronger brethren.
So La Fontaine, the great French fable-writer, found,
as Taine has brilliantly demonstrated, the prototypes
of his animals at the court of Louis XIV.   Under the
guise of the Lion he suggested the characteristics of the
king of France, and under the masks of the various birds
and beasts those of his courtiers.   So also Rostand, in
his 'Chantecler' — a play which could never have been
written without a knowledge of the medieval Reynard
stories — has incidentally satirized the affectations of

the present day. When the Guinea-Hen gives an af-
ternoon tea, we recognize in her conversation and in
that of her guests a reflection of the frivolous and vapid
talk of modern circles of shallow culture and vacuous
self-satisfaction. The man who tells an animal tale
as it should be told, with plenty of local color and
characterization drawn from real life, can hardly escape
constructing an allegory of his own times. If we have
the wit to read between the lines, we can gather from
such tales much of the social history of the period.

This is precisely what happened in the Middle Ages.
With the beginning of the feudal period, these simple
folk-tales, which had long been current in oral form,
and as fables and apologs among more learned circles,
began to assume a more elaborate shape. More and
more they came to reflect the life and manners of men,
and more and more, as they expanded, they grew in
dramatic interest. They were now no longer brief,
making a single situation effective; they ran to considerable length, narrating a whole series of events,
with the added interest of suspense. They became epic,
in the larger sense of the word. Their heroes and
heroines began to assume personalities as definite as
those in any epic poem, and these distinctive characteristics were crystallized in appropriate names, —
Reynard and Couart and Isengrim, instead of The Fox
or The Hare or The Wolf. Such figures, in their larger
epic capacity, became as familiar to the people as
Roland or Ganelon. But while the characteristics of
Roland or Ganelon were derived from tradition, in
which the one had proved himself a hero and the other,
in no wise connected with him, a traitor, the charac-

teristics of Reynard or Isengrim were determined and
corrected by actual observation of the traits and habits
of the fox and the wolf. The human elements constantly tended to increase, however. The more popular
these animals became as epic figures, the more they
acted like men and the less they behaved like beasts.
We see them worship like Christians, go to mass, ride on
horses, debate at length in councils, and divert themselves with hawking and hunting. And the elaboration
of the story, involving a close portrayal of manners and
customs, brought with it real or implied comment on
these ear-marks of the age. Satire creeps in, even in
the earlier versions, and in the later versions is often
carried to an inartistic excess. While generally gay
and good-humored, these more elaborate beast-stories
are sometimes overweighted by their gibes at individuals
or at social abuses. The point of some of these jests is
plain enough at the present day. When the Fox, whom
we all know to be a villain, confesses his sins to the
Badger, with much mouthing of Latin prayers, or vows
he will go to the Holy Land on a pious pilgrimage, we
know that the man who inserted these satirical elaborations in the story had his own ideas about the sincerity
of religious observances in his own day. Or, to take
another instance, when the Camel rises to address the
court before which Reynard is on trial, and speaks lame
legal French with a strong Italian accent, we can
recognize a hit at certain Italian lawyers who meddled
in French politics. Often, however, the allegory is not
clear enough, or our knowledge of contemporary events
minute enough, to penetrate the subtleties of the animal
disguises. The face of an individual may be hidden

beneath the mask of the brute, but it is generally too cleverly hidden and too soon withdrawn for recognition.

It must never be forgotten that the medieval stories about Reynard the Fox do not form a single well-proportioned and consistent whole. Even in France, where they attained their greatest brilliancy and spirit, they were far from being all cast in the same mold. They are, as has just been suggested, often called an epic, but if we put them together, we shall have no such poem as the 'Song of Roland' or 'Beowulf.' They reflect the ideas of different men and the society of different times and places. They are not similar in structure, or of equal literary merit. Indecorous episodes and irrelevant additions abound. In later times the simple country landscape in which the beasts had moved was even, in one version, mixed up with the walls of windy Troy. Still later, the tales got into prose form, as in the version which Caxton printed for English readers about the time of the Discovery of America, more than three centuries after the beast-tale had begun to assume epic proportions in Western Europe. During these centuries we must think of the adventures of Reynard as spreading, in this more elaborate form, through France and Holland and Flanders and Germany and England. Out of all this mass of stories it is hard to say which shall be called the true romance of Reynard, which of all these profane gospels shall be held canonical.

There is, however, a certain unity about the great medieval collection made on French soil and known as the 'Roman de Renart.' Although the separate stories of which it is composed are of varying age and pro-

venience, they preserve a certain symmetry, a certain
regard for the spirit of the work as a whole. These
different "branches," as they are called, have often
been likened to the branches of a tree, some of which
have grown strong and large, and are burdened with
leaves and fruit, while others, of slighter growth, have
burgeoned in a later spring, and are overshadowed by
their stouter neighbors. And just as the limbs of
a tree should not be too symmetrical, too exactly
balanced, but ought to give, by their very irregularity,
an impression of unstudied beauty, so the "branches"
of this poem produce a certain effect upon the reader
by their unlikeness, by their variety and contrast. It
is this collection which we shall take for our discussion
here, since it represents the beast-epic in its best medieval estate, without the exaggerations of the later versions.

The Fox is the hero of the medieval beast-epic, in fact
as well as in name. He holds the center of the stage;
there are few episodes in which he does not appear.
Upon his figure is lavished the most brilliant characterization, and his actions are made the occasion for the
sharpest satire. He is preëminent among all the beasts
for cunning and rascality. By the pure exercise of his
wits he prevails over those stronger than himself in mere
physical endowment. But a certain poetic justice is
preserved ; when Reynard attempts to injure the weaker
creatures, he is likely to come off second best. Clever
as he is, the Tom-tit and the Cock outwit him. "Let
me give you the kiss of peace!" he says to the Tom-
tit on the branch over his head. "By my faith," replies the Tom-tit, "I'll do it!" But the bird has seen

through the trick, and at the moment when the Fox tries to snap her up, he gets a "handful" of moss and leaves which the Tom-tit has gathered, full in his face and eyes. In the well-known story of his capture of Chanticleer, so charmingly told by Chaucer, he loses his prey through the superior cunning of the Cock. The hero of the animal tales is not always successful, by any means. Brer Rabbit has his misfortunes; the Turkey Buzzard and the Terrapin prove too much for his wits, and, as we have seen, he loses his tail in the ice. But these are the exceptions; both Brer Rabbit and Reynard seldom get worsted. It is curious, on the other hand, that the chief place for cleverness is given by the negroes to the timorous and ineffectual rabbit. In the Middle Ages, Couart, "the coward," as he is called, is no match for the Fox. On one occasion he is so scared by Reynard that he has a two-days' fever. We can better understand why the python Kaa has such a store of wisdom among the beasts of Kipling's jungle, or why the Germans of to-day exalt the dachshund, whose exploits you may see set forth in almost any number of the 'Fliegende Blätter.' But Brer Rabbit is perhaps effective through his very weakness. If a hero accomplishes as much as he de-spite such severe handicaps, is he not twice a hero? And he serves better the gentler humor of the negroes, while the mordant cynicism and the delight in sheer deviltry of the 'Romance of Reynard' are better brought out by a protagonist like the rascally Fox.

Reynard is one of the most picturesque villains in the whole range of fiction, as subtle and hypocritical as Tartuffe, as dashing and debonair as Don Juan, as

heartless as Iago, and always as whimsically lawless
as Dick Turpin.   He is nobody's friend, and yet he is
the constant associate of the other animals.   They all
have a grievance against him, and yet he can bask in
the sun in front of his residence, the famous "fortress"
of Maleperduys, and pass the time of day with them
as they walk by.   He can take refuge from their righteous wrath in the secret passages and tortuous windings
of this abode, but he much prefers the excitement of
trusting to his own ingenuity.   Nothing pleases him
better than to see how close to the wind he can sail.
He has something of the same intellectual delight in
his villainy that Shakspere's Richard III displays.
Richard's winning of Lady Anne is hardly more a piece
of virtuosity than the process by which the Fox makes
the Raven, sitting on the branch over his head, drop the
piece of cheese he covets.   In this old story, common
from the days of Æsop to those of La Fontaine, the
'Romance of Reynard' shows a subtlety and a distinction of treatment which put it in a class by itself.
The Raven does not hold the cheese in his beak, as in
the classic fable; he has it securely between his claws.
This makes the task of the Fox far more difficult; he is
obliged to work up his effect by degrees.   First a start of
pleased surprise at seeing his "compère" on the branch
above him, then a reflection on the musical skill of the
Raven's sainted father.   The Fox further recalls that
the Raven used to sing in his infancy, and, as a lover
of music, he begs him to sing a little now.   So the
flattered bird croaks out a few notes.   "You're in even
better voice than usual," says the Fox.   "See if you
can't take one note higher."   The Raven obligingly com-

plies, but the cheese does not fall. "God!" says Reynard, "what purity of tone! If you only keep yourself
in condition, you'll be the first singer of the age. Do
sing *once* more!" And the Raven, in his excitement,
drops the cheese. But even then Reynard waits for
a further effect, and heroically refrains from eating
the tempting morsel immediately in the hope of getting
the Raven for a meal too. He almost succeeds in entic-
ing him off his branch by pretending that the cheese,
in falling, has hurt his leg. In this he is unsuccessful,
although the Raven has a close shave in escaping. But
Reynard has the satisfaction of eating the cheese before
the eyes of the discomfited bird, "and he didn't com-
plain that it made a bad meal."

The 'Romance of Reynard' appeals to the eternal
sympathy with a successful rascal latent in human
nature; the same quality which endears Punch to
our hearts, despite his ghastly catalogue of crimes, or
secures the popularity of dramas of roguery, from
'Peck's Bad Boy' to 'Raffles.' No attempt is made
to excuse the actions of the Fox; that would have
spoiled the fun. This is done elsewhere, however;
Caxton avows that he relates such deceits "not to the
intent that men should use them, but that every man
should eschew and keep him from the subtle false
shrews that they be not deceived," — which reminds us
of Defoe's pious justification of his stories of rakes and
courtesans as awful warnings, a sanctimonious pose
which has never made them less piquant from that day
to this. Nor is there any attempt in the 'Roman de
Renart' to do justice on the villain, even though he is
sometimes discomfited. Its spirit is much like that of

Uncle Remus.   When Brer Possum is burned to death
through the devices of Brer Rabbit, Uncle Remus observes, "In dis worruld lots er fokes is gotter suffer fer
odder fokes sins."

Professor Brander Matthews has called attention to
Kipling's imaginative power in creating for his beasts
a special Law of the Jungle, and has pointed out that
"it is this portrayal of wild life subject to an immiti-
gable code which gives its sustaining moral to the narrative of Mowgli's career."   But both in the creation of
a special Law of Beasts and in the addition of a moral
application, Kipling has departed from the popular
beast-tale.   Such stories have, indeed, in the shape of
fables and the like, often been made directly didactic,
but they have pointed morals of everyday human life,
they have not been designed to illustrate special codes
of ethics among animals.   While the beast-tales of the
Middle Ages set forth a system of government, it is not
a system peculiar to animals, but a reflection of the laws
of men.   One "branch" of the 'Romance of Reynard'
affords an admirable illustration of this.   Here we
are shown the beasts assembled at the court of their
king, and the royal methods of dispensing justice.
There is little in it really distinctive of the beast-world.
It is a bitter satire on the capriciousness of kings, the
miscarriages of justice, the windy eloquence of counselors, and the abuses of religious observance.   We
cannot do better than examine this famous scene a little
in detail.

King Noble the Lion is holding his court, at which
all the animals have assembled, save Reynard the Fox.
The proceedings are opened by Isengrim the Wolf, who

rises to demand justice against Reynard, whose flirta-
tions with the Wolf's spouse, Dame Hersent, have
passed all bounds of propriety. The Lion smiles
cynically, and tells him he is making too much of a
small matter. The king has no intention of interfer-
ing in the feud between the two, nor is he inclined to
change his mind when Bruin the Bear implores him to
make peace between his "barons." The lady protests
her innocence with many blushes, swearing "by all the
saints whom she adores," and hints that Isengrim is
unreasonably jealous. Others speak, but the king's
will is inflexible; despite the manifest sins of Reynard
he snubs Isengrim again, who is obliged to sit down in
discomfiture, with his tail between his legs. But suddenly the scene changes; the Hen Pinte is brought in
on a bier, terribly mangled by the teeth of the Fox.
Her sisters and Chanticleer the Cock, filling the air with
their lamentations, act as escort. Chanticleer, bathing
the king's feet with his tears, sets forth the harrowing
details of this latest crime of Reynard; the Hens fall
swooning to the ground, and great excitement ensues.
The "barons" demand vengeance in the high heroic
style; the monarch, as a man of sensibility, is profoundly moved, and consents to summon the Fox to
appear at court and answer for his misdeeds. But the
ambassadors whom he sends, Bruin and Tybert the
Cat, return torn and bleeding, outwitted by the cleverness of the Fox. Finally Grimbert the Badger, bearing the royal seal, succeeds in fetching him. Reynard
trembles as he reads the summons, and wishes that he
were in a position to have the consolations of religion,
though he adds that he hasn't much of an opinion of

monks. "Never mind!" says Grimbert, "confess
your sins to me." This the Fox does, and Grimbert
gives him absolution. On the next morning, he takes
a tearful leave of his wife, and bids his children remember their high lineage, and guard well his castle. He
also sends up a petition to the Almighty to strengthen
him in the approaching struggle. Arrived at the court,
he finds all the animals arrayed against him, but he is
no coward, and defends himself in a most eloquent
speech. The king is unmoved, however. "You talk
well, but you are a traitor," he says, and Reynard is
condemned to death. There are none so poor to do
him reverence; even the Monkey makes faces at him.
The scaffold is raised, and now Reynard braces himself
for a supreme effort, — he informs the king that he has
repented of his sins, and that he desires to go on a
pilgrimage to the Holy Land. The monarch is touched
with pity, and on this condition grants him the royal
pardon. The queen presents him with a ring; and
amidst the mutterings of all the other animals, he sets
out, in pilgrim's weeds, ostensibly to begin his long
journey then and there. But once safe outside the
court he defies the monarch, flings aside his pilgrim's
attire, and escapes to his comfortable dinner in the
fortress of Maleperduys.

Only the barest outlines of the scene have been
given; it is impossible to suggest the wealth of incident, the deftness of the characterization, the brilliancy of the satire. As Léopold Sudre observes, "No
parody of the manners of the times, of feudal usages,
of those solemn and terrible trials at the end of which
a knight saved his life by going to the Holy Land,

surpasses this in pungency and subtlety." It will be noted that the method of treatment, despite the elaborations, is in many respects close to that of the popular beast-tale. The idea of assembling the animals in council before their king is of course very common. Uncle Remus for one knows all about such gatherings. "En w'en de Lion shuck his mane, and tuck his seat in de big cheer, den de sesshun begun fer ter commence." His animals act just as men would do — "dey spoke speeches, en hollered, en cusst, en flung der langwidge roun' des like w'en yo' daddy wuz gwineter run fer de legislater en got lef'." The difference in the attitude of Mowgli's companions is perfectly clear. They despise the laws of human beings, and have social and legal arrangements of their own,— or rather of Kipling's own. In the 'Romance of Reynard,' on the other hand, which conforms in this respect far better to the truly popular type of beast-literature, the Law of the Jungle is a travesty of human institutions.

Reynard is a thoroughly French creation; he is English only by adoption. He is the embodiment of all the deviltry in the Gallic character, reduced to its quintessence, and vivified in animal form. Jusserand sees in him the progenitor of a long line of admirable rascals, — Panurge, Scapin, Figaro. "Reynard is the first of the family; he is such a natural and spontaneous creation of the French mind that we see him appearing from century to century, the same character under different names." His figure derives its extraordinary piquancy from the brilliancy of Gallic humor. The French imposed their ideal rascal upon their brother nations as easily as they did their ideal heroes. To their fostering care Reynard owed his reputation as much as Arthur did, although the French were no more responsible for his origin than they were for the presence of the historical Welsh leader on the shores of sixth-century Britain. Reynard was but a wanderer upon the face of the earth when the French took him to their hearts, and if he proved an unruly child before they were done with him, he also proved faithful to the traditions of the race which reared him.

What, then, is the significance of his adventures for the development of the English nation? If he is so thoroughly French in all his characteristics, why ought we to study his exploits rather than those of an English hero?

The answer is perhaps obvious enough. At the time when this story was assuming its characteristic "epic" form, a considerable part of the English people were of French blood. The British Isles were of course full of Frenchmen who were a little later to be merged in the newer nation. The dominions of the king of England lay partly in France, and certain "branches" of the 'Romance of Reynard' were composed in these continental possessions of the English sovereigns. Intercourse between the two nations was constant and intimate. The literature of England from the Conquest to Chaucer is, of course, not necessarily in the English tongue. With the exception of Latin, French was supreme, and few productions in the vernacular during this period were uninfluenced by French models. The English metrical romances, for example, with scarcely an exception, were either directly translated or adapted from the French. The 'Romance of Reynard,' then, is almost as significant for England as for France, since it was the production of an integral part of the future English people. It is significant also as the expression of a general tendency in western European literature, first manifested in France, and given most dramatic expression in that country. In outlining this general tendency we are also summing up the spirit of the beast-epic, and revealing the deepest significance of its allegory.

'Reynard the Fox' is the epic of disillusionment. It satirizes everybody and everything; nothing is safe from its mocking laughter. It forms a complete antithesis to the idealism of the Arthurian romances. The lofty resolves, the gentle acts, the finer social conventions of the system of chivalry are here burlesqued. The scene just outlined, for example, reduces to absurdity the ardor which found expression in the Crusades and in the legends of the Holy Grail. What becomes of religious fervor here? It is only the trick by which the rascally Fox cheats justice, hoodwinks the king, and saves his own skin. What is religion? A rhapsody of words, which the villain is glad enough to patter over in bad Latin with a wink and a grin. What is heroism? Stealing and not getting caught. What becomes of the purity of woman? The ludicrous figure of Dame Hersent, the she-wolf, guilty enough, but blushing and protesting, accusing her husband of jealousy, but unwilling to have her virtue too closely examined. Reminiscences of the national epic, too, are made to heighten the fun. King Noble tears his mane, as Charlemagne did his white beard, and when he exclaims to his barons, "O God, counsel me! What

devilishness do I hear of this Reynard who has so
deceived me! And I can find no one to avenge me on
this foe!" we hear an echo of the entreaties of Charlemagne to avenge the death of Roland on the traitor
Ganelon. Even the hero of the epic is himself ridiculed, as we have seen; he is deceived by the Raven
and the Tom-tit and the Cock. If the story is epic in
its breadth, then, it is all-embracing in its cynicism.
"The unholy Bible of the world," one critic calls it,
and indeed it is Holy Writ and every other sacred
tradition turned wrong side out. It is not always
bitter; the satire is more often genial. But it can take
nothing with reverence; it cannot relax for a moment
its grin of humorous disbelief in the better motives of
mankind. Traces of this attitude meet us on every
hand in the Middle Ages; even religion, with all its
terrors, could not banish it. Men might be doomed to
hell-fire, but they sometimes took pleasure in making
faces at the devil, and occasionally performing a similar
trick before the Deity. So even in the churches Reynard and others of his kind leer out at us from the pages
of illuminated missals, or from the carvings of miserere-
stalls, where monks were wont to kneel in the most
impassioned of all supplications to an unrelenting God.
The 'Romance of Reynard' is the quintessence of that
mocking spirit, the reaction against the overstrained
idealism of the system of chivalry. We have seen that
this system carried with it much that made for greater
refinement and a better social consciousness. But it
left in its wake a revolt in the direction of materialism
and realism. Men perceived the cupidity and hypocrisy of many of those who had declared their allegiance

to those ideals.   In France this spirit of disillusion was expressed by the ' Romance of Reynard.'   In England, as we shall see in the next chapter, the Saxon elements in the community uttered their protest through the "proud outlaw" Robin Hood.

VII

THE BALLADS OF ROBIN HOOD

Under the greenwood tree
Who loves to lie with me,
And turn his merry note
Unto the sweet bird's throat,
Come hither, come hither, come hither !
Here shall he see
No enemy
But winter and rough weather.
                              — Shakspere.

VII

THE BALLADS OF ROBIN HOOD

As patriotic Americans, we are accustomed to speak with a certain pride of the achievements of American poets. We point to the graceful verses of Longfellow, the iridescent lyrics of Poe, the rugged lines of Whitman, and the brilliant satire of Lowell, as worthy to stand beside the best which the mother-country has produced during the Victorian era. For the work of such men as these and of a host of minor poets we have abundant appreciation. But only within a short time have we taken any notice at all of a most interesting and characteristic variety of American verse, — the songs of the Western cowboys. These men, living together on the solitary ranches of Texas, Arizona, or New Mexico, have been accustomed to entertain each other after the day's work is done by singing songs, some of which have been familiar to them from boyhood, others of which they have actually composed themselves. Their ballads are rude poetry, made with no thought of literary effect, but they have a charm of their own; they pulse with mounting rhythms, and they almost run to melody even without the accompanying music. The separate stanzas are sometimes followed by a refrain, in which the entire listening com-

171

pany may join.   The subjects of the songs are varied,
— the joys and sorrows of the cowboy's profession,
the exploits of bold adventurers, the checkered course
of true love, — but the sentiment seldom degenerates
into sentimentality, and the vigor rarely becomes bombast.   It is the verse of a freer life than that of the
dweller in cities, and it betrays its origin in its rugged
sincerity.

> I'm a rowdy cowboy just off the stormy plains,
> My trade is girting saddles and pulling bridle reins,
> Oh, I can tip the lasso, it is with graceful ease;
> I rope a streak of lightning, and ride it where I please.
> My bosses they all like me, they say I am hard to beat;
> I give them the bold standoff, you bet I have got the cheek.
> I always work for wages, my pay I get in gold;
> I am bound to follow the longhorn steer until I am too old.
>   Ci yi yip yip yip pe ya.[1]

These ballads may fairly claim special attention,
not only because they are produced by Americans on
American soil, and because they treat of native themes,
but because they have been composed under exceptional circumstances.   Most American poetry, like
most verse of the present day, reflects in a very high
degree the impressions of the individual poet.   This
is as true of such men as Walt Whitman and his
followers as of anybody; Whitman's work was intensely subjective, though he felt himself to be a
mouthpiece of universal human experience.   These
cowboy ballads, on the other hand, are not the expres-
sions of individuals, but of the whole company which
listens to them, and they are, in a very real sense, the

[1] John A. Lomax, *Cowboy Songs*, New York, 1910, p. 310.

work of other men than the author. "Whatever the
most gifted man could produce must bear the criticism
of the entire camp, and agree with the ideas of a group
of men.   In this sense, therefore, any song that came
from such a group would be the joint product of a
number of them, telling perhaps the story of some
stampede they had all fought to turn, some crime in
which they had all shared equally, some comrade's
tragic death which they had all witnessed."   The
author counts for nothing, it will be observed; his
name is generally not remembered, and what he invents
is as characteristic of his comrades as of himself.   The
lines celebrating the career of Bill Peters, the stage
driver, are fairly typical.

> Bill Peters was a hustler
> From Independence town;
> He warn't a college scholar
> Nor man of great renown,
> But Bill had a way o' doing things
> And doin' 'em up brown.
>
> Bill driv the stage from Independence
> Up to the Smoky Hill;
> And everybody knowed him thar
> As Independence Bill, —
> Thar warn't no feller on the route
> That driv with half the skill.
>
> *   *   *   *   *
>
> The way them wheels 'u'd rattle,
> And the way the dust 'u'd fly,
> You'd think a million cattle
> Had stampeded and gone by;
> But the mail 'u'd get thar just the same,
> If the horses had to die.

He driv that stage for many a year
Along the Smoky Hill,
And a pile o' wild Comanches
Did Bill Peters have to kill, —
And I reckon if he'd had good luck
He'd been a drivin' still.

But he chanced one day to run agin
A bullet made o' lead,
Which was harder than he bargained for,
And now poor Bill is dead;
And when they brung his body home
A barrel of tears was shed.

Here we have literature which is a perfect index of the social ideals of the body of men among whom it is composed, literature which makes no pretense to literary form or to disclosure of the emotions of any one man as distinguished from his fellows. There are few communities of the present day which are as closely united in common aims and sympathies as these bands of Western cowboys, hence there are few opportunities for the production of verse which is as truly the expression of universal emotions as are these songs.

Such Western ranches reproduce almost perfectly the conditions under which the English popular ballads were composed. Among the country folk of England in the old days there was the same spontaneous desire to tell a story in song, — a desire as old as humanity itself, — the same absence of conscious art in the making of these songs, the same picturesque vigor of narration. The ballads were meant to be sung, as is shown by the refrains, which were sometimes meaningless, a mere accompaniment to the tune, like the "ci

yi yip yip yip pe ya" of the cowboy song, sometimes a
sort of chorus, emphasizing the point of the story itself.
There was none of the appeal of the printed page to
the eye of the reader upon which modern verse relies
so much for its effect.   They were the songs of any man
and of every man, written indeed by some individual,
but not thought of as his work, hardly existing until
accepted by the community as a whole, and altered
at will by any of the members of this community.
Thus the old English ballads were, just like the cowboy songs, reflections of the ideals of those who produced them, and they afford most valuable testimony
to the social development of people in the lower walks
of life.

We all know how much influence these communal
ballads have exerted upon the poetry of conscious art.
Wordsworth, Coleridge, Keats, Longfellow, Morris, Ros-
setti, all learned much from the ballads, and a multitude of lesser men have been profoundly affected by
them.   It is a curious thing that direct imitations have
seldom been successful; it is as difficult to reproduce
precisely the effect of verse composed under conditions
which rarely exist at the present day as it is for a gar-
dener to suggest, by artificial cultivation, the unspoiled
charm of nature in the woods and fields.   Two men
have, in different ways, achieved the greatest measure
of success in ballad-writing, two men whom we have
already noted as possessing something of the medieval
temper, — Scott and Kipling.   Sir Walter went to
school to ballad-poetry as a boy, and his later work is
full of its swinging rhythms and its picturesque phrases.
He could counterfeit it, too, in such a masterly way

that no one can tell, at the present day, how much of the "emended" ballad of 'Kinmont Willie' which he printed in his 'Minstrelsy of the Scottish Border,' is due to him and how much to tradition. Kipling has proceeded in a different fashion. He has set forth in ballad-verse the emotions of a distinct class, the British soldiery. Tommy Atkins is the whole army of privates and petty officers rolled into one, and what he sings in the barrack-room comes very close to the universality of the ballads of the medieval English peasantry or of the Texas cowboys. He and his comrades are intellectually on much the same plane as their British ancestors or their American neighbors; Bill 'Awkins is first cousin to Kinmont Willie and Bill Peters. Although coming from the pen of a man of letters, this expression of the thoughts and aspirations of the British soldier demands, through its sympathetic understanding, almost as much attention as if it had actually come from members of the class it describes.

The ballads of Robin Hood are much simpler than most of the verse which we have been considering. We have generally been obliged to look at popular stories in their more sophisticated forms, stories which were once out in the open country, but which have in time become the property of the higher classes of society. We have always tried to follow these stories back into their simpler forms; we have seen how fairy-tales show the earlier stages of the story of Beowulf and the demon Grendel, or how old Celtic narratives reveal the pagan beginnings of the Quest of the Holy Grail, and we have observed that the origins of the story of Roland are to be sought among the people.

But we have seldom been able to get at these earlier versions in a satisfactory way. Here, however, in the Robin Hood ballads, we have the actual beginnings of a great story among the folk, not its transformation at the hands of more cultured men. For once, we are at the fountainhead of song, rather than beside the brimming river of epic.

It is from such songs as these that an epic is made, however, partly by the natural combination of a number of these into a group, but mainly by the alterations and additions of some one gifted poet, who has the courage to do what he chooses with the narrative material before him, rejecting here, amplifying there, — in brief, shaping what was formerly ill-ordered and inconsistent into a well-rounded whole. While he may preserve much of the popular character of this material, he makes of it something different, something artistic. But the hand of such a craftsman as molded 'Beowulf' or the 'Song of Roland' or the 'Nibelungenlied' has never touched the ballads. An effort has indeed been made to combine certain of them in the long ballad, or rather collection of ballads, called 'The Gest of Robin Hood.' Here we have a variety of pieces set end for end, with some care for transition and order. But this reveals the timid prentice hand of a country fellow, trying vaguely to do something to which the ballad-singing folk were unaccustomed. The simple ballad they understood; they were unprepared for the fuller narrative of epic, which requires a greater art than theirs, an art where the poet of superior attainment steps in, and addresses an audience of different character.

The chief reason, perhaps, why the Robin Hood ballads were never worked up into elaborate epic form is that by their very nature they would make no appeal to that more exalted class of society which welcomes an epic on the grand scale. Robin Hood's chief energies, as we shall see, were directed towards righting the abuses inflicted by the upper classes on those of lower social station. Consequently his exploits appealed only to the common people; the upper classes would not have felt enthusiastic about perpetuating them. The case was quite different with such a hero as Arthur, who, a popular champion, was revered in the beginning as a national figure, and not as the representative of any one class of society. There were indeed no such clearly marked social divisions in the old days when Arthur led the Celts to victory as there were when Robin Hood came into existence. It was possible for Arthur later on to become a paragon of chivalry, the ideal of the upper classes, because his figure was so shadowy that any use could easily be made of it. He had no individuality beyond his successes in war. Not so with Robin Hood. His whole existence depended upon his character as a "proud outlaw," and nothing could make him into a conventional member of society. Born as a hero of the common people, he always retained that distinction, and he never could have lost it without forfeiting everything which made him recognizable as an individual. Can we imagine him putting off the Lincoln green and dwelling in happiness in the royal court? The ballads tell us that he once tried it, and was restless until he could resume his former life

once more. He was no subject for a stately epic, —
not even for one of the semi-primitive type of the
'Song of Roland.' He belongs, not in the close air of
courts, but out of doors, in the midst of the common
people.

Robin Hood is in no sense a historical character.
The incarnation of democratic revolt, as Sigurd was the
embodiment of valor, he was born, not of human parents, but of the imagination of the English peasantry.
He was an outlaw, because he was created to typify
resistance to abuses of the law. There is something
about an outlaw which has always appealed to popular
sympathy. The bold man who plays a desperate and
dangerous game, with the organized forces of society
against him, exercises a singular fascination over us
all. We have had occasion to observe this in the
romance of 'Reynard the Fox.' The Western cowboys delight in celebrating such heroes as Jesse
James, or Cole Younger, the bank robber. Something
more than mere delight in dashing outlawry has gone
to the making of the figure of Robin Hood, however,
— he typifies above all else the protest of the English
people against social injustice; he voices the growing
independence of the commons.

These ballads impress us first, not by their protest,
but by their picturesqueness. The action takes place
in the open air, sometimes in the depths of the forest,
with the deer and the fawns peeping shyly through the
trees, sometimes on the highroad, sometimes in a
woodland glade, where a feast is spread on the green
grass, and the arching branches overhead make a
vaulted banqueting-hall more majestic than any that

the king can claim. It is always summer; there is no
suggestion of the rigors of winter, or the possible in-
conveniences of the soaking English rains to woodland
rovers. Again and again the beautiful lines recur, in
varying forms : —

> In somer, when the shawes be sheyne,
>   And leves be large and long,
> Hit is ful mery in feyre foreste
>   To here the foulys song:
>
> To se the dere draw to the dale,
>   And leve the hilles hee,
> And shadow hem in the levës grene,
>   Under the grene-wode tree.

The whole tone of the ballads is in keeping with this
charming background. They are cheerful verse; everything is "merry," even the priory where Robin Hood
meets his death ! England is "merry," Sherwood
forest is "merry," and Robin himself is "merry as
bird on bough," for the charm of the woodlands is
as potent with him as with us. All this enthusiasm
for the woodland life, for hunting and feasting, for
archery and for rustic sports, is not mere decoration;
it is an important part of the story. If ever verse
lashed abuses with a smile, it is this. The sun shines
brightly overhead; it is a good world to be alive in, its
wrongs are being righted, and its very misfortunes are
ultimately to bring happier times.

Robin leads an adventurous life, but there is a certain sameness about his experiences, as related in the
single ballads. He is always meeting some adversary
whose strength and courage are sufficient excuse for
arranging a good fight on the spot, to prove which of

them is the better man.   The stout stranger may be a
tanner or a tinker or a shepherd or a clouted beggar,
and sometimes he gets the best of it, and Robin is
beaten.   But it is noticeable that if the hero is overcome in one of these struggles, it is by one of the common people, not by a man of the despised upper classes.
The defeat of Robin Hood belongs rather to subsequent tradition.   It is a curious fact that later
generations often lose faith in a great hero, and
like to see him come to grief.   Many of these
ballads are too late and fantastic to be treated as part
of the same impulse which produced the earlier specimens.   When Robin Hood wearies of chasing the fallow
deer and resolves to go to Scarborough and become a
fisherman, or when he forsakes Sherwood forest and
wanders into the unreal land of romance to fight with
the Prince of Aragon, while Little John makes things
uncomfortable for a giant, — then it is time to take
leave of him and his merry men.

It is better for us to fix our attention on the 'Gest
of Robin Hood,' that curious poem, too long to be
called a ballad, too short and crude to be called an
epic, yet on its way to epic form because it narrates a
story of some length and elaboration centering about
a single figure, and in a heroic rather than a romantic
vein.   Here Robin appears at his very best, less a mere
swashbuckler holding the open championship of merry
England in a free-for-all fight, and more a person of
character and reflection and convictions about the inequalities of society.   As far as it goes, it sets forth
what is most worth while in the life of Robin Hood
down to the time of his death.   It does not bother

to invent a birth and boyhood for him, as one of the
inferior later ballads does ; it introduces him to us immediately as "standing in Bernesdale," leaning against
a tree. The 'Gest' is right; that is the way that
Robin was born, full-grown and clad in Lincoln green,
sprung out of the depths of the forest, like Minerva
full-armed from the head of Jove. The ablest of his
yeomen were Little John, Much the miller's son, and
Scarlet or Scathelock. Not until later did such characters as Allen a Dale, Maid Marian, and Friar Tuck
join the band. There is no occasion for Robin Hood
to feel that his company is too small, however; he has
seven score of these sturdy yeomen to do his bidding,
amply sufficient to make him indeed a man to be feared
by all who cross his path.

The moment the curtain rises, we find Robin itch-
ing for an adventure. He cannot get up an appetite
for dinner until he has forced some wealthy malefactor
to share his meal, and pay well for it afterwards.
Before his desire is satisfied, we are told a good deal
about his character. This is doubly significant, because
it is not the habit of the ballads to dwell much on personal description; they are far more concerned with
deeds. But Robin Hood was no ordinary outlaw; he
was careful of religious observances, he never sat down
to dine until he had heard three masses, one in honor
of the Father, another in honor of the Holy Ghost,
and the third in honor of the Virgin Mary. Although
he plundered "fat-headed" and fat-pursed monks, he
was no infidel. He loved the Virgin so much that he
would never harm any company in which there was a
woman. He was always courteous; of this we are re-

minded again and again.   His character is still further
set forth in the instructions which he gives to Little
John.

> "Maistar," than sayde Lytil Johnn,
> "And we our borde shal sprede,
> Tel us wheder that we shal go,
> And what life that we shall lede.

> "Where we shall take, where we shall leve,
> Where we shall abide behynde,
> Where we shall robbe, where we shall reve,
> Where we shall bete and bynde."

> "Thereof no force," than sayde Robyn;
> "We shall do well inowe;
> But loke ye do no husbonde harme,
> That tilleth with his ploughe.

> "No more ye shall no gode yeman
> That walketh by grenë-wode shawe;
> Ne no knyght ne no squyer
> That wol be a gode felawe.

> "These bisshopes and these arche-bisshopes,
> Ye shall them bete and bynde;
> The hye sherif of Notyingham,
> Hym holde ye in your mynde."

> "This worde shal be holde," sayde Lytell Johnn,
> "And this lesson we shall lere;
> It is fer dayes; God send us a gest,
> That we were at oure dynere!"

Presently a stranger comes riding by. He is a
knight, but no proud and haughty warrior; on the
contrary, his hood is falling over his eyes, one foot
dangles carelessly from the stirrup, everything about

him indicates the deepest dejection.   Little John welcomes him to the greenwood and invites him to dine with his master.   After a bounteous meal of bread and wine and venison and all kinds of game, Robin suggests that he pay for his entertainment, but the knight replies that he has but ten shillings to his name.   Little John prudently tests the truth of this statement, but finds only just this sum in the knight's coffers.   Robin refuses to take so small an amount, and inquires the reason of his guest's gloomy demeanor.   The knight replies that he owes four hundred pounds to a rich abbot, that he has been obliged to pledge his lands in satisfaction of the debt, and that his friends have all failed him.   The sympathies of the robbers are touched; Robin offers to lend him the money himself.   So the knight goes rejoicing on his way to settle the debt, with a new gown and horse, new boots and spurs, and Little John acting as escort.   The next scene is in the abbot's hall.   The knight pleads earnestly with the abbot and with the justice and the high sheriff of Nottingham to grant him an extension of time.   He offers to serve the abbot, but all to no purpose; the abbot orders him to leave.

> "Out," he sayde, "thou falsë knyght,
>   Spede the out of my hall!"

Then, just at the dramatic moment, the knight produces his four hundred pounds, and settles the debt. He then goes home with a light heart, and in due course of time gets sufficient money to repay Robin Hood.

Meanwhile, the outlaws have been having various

adventures. The time for the repayment of the money
is at hand, and again Little John goes forth to stop
travelers on the highway, that his master may not lack
a guest for dinner. This time two black monks fall
into the net, one of whom proves to be the "high
cellarer" of the very abbey which had treated the good
knight so shamefully. Little John discovers more than
eight hundred pounds in his coffers, which is duly
transferred to the greenwood treasury.

> "Grete well your abbot," sayd Robyn,
>   "And your pryour, I you pray,
> And byd hym sende me such a monke
>   To dyner every day."

The knight now appears, with apologies for his late-
ness, — he has been helping a poor yeoman, who was
being ill-treated. He offers to pay his debt, but
Robin refuses to take his money, saying that he has
already received it from the high cellarer of the abbey.
Moreover, he insists that the knight shall take the extra
four hundred pounds which the monk has just been
forced to surrender. And so, with good wishes on
either side, Robin and the knight take leave of each
other.

Here Robin appears not only as the champion of the
distressed and needy, but as the enemy of rich and
unprincipled ecclesiastics. The churchmen always get
but scant consideration in these ballads. They are
not only in possession of much ill-gotten wealth ; they
are uncharitable and discourteous. The abbot dis-
misses the knight with insult ; the black monks in the
forest treat Robin with incivility. It is interesting
to see such purely popular literature as this insisting

so much on courtesy. The ideals of the aristocracy have filtered down to the lower classes; the heroes of romance no longer have a monopoly of politeness, they share it with the champions of popular story. Again, it is significant that Robin Hood does not spare the monks, although they belong to the abbey of St. Mary the Virgin, his patron saint. Even if they have dedicated themselves to the service of Our Lady, they are so false and treacherous as to deserve no mercy. Nothing reveals more strikingly than this the intense hatred which the common people felt for the wealthy religious orders.

But the arch-enemy of Robin Hood is the high sheriff of Nottingham, the representative of the law in the particular district in which Robin resides. Taken against his will and forced to dine with Robin in the forest, the sheriff has a most uncomfortable time. He is forced to see the greenwood feast decorated with silver vessels stolen from his own table, and to spend the night in the open air. The ballad takes a certain delight in the humor of the situation.

> All nyght lay the proudë sherif
>   In his breche and in his schert;
> No wonder it was, in grenë wode,
>   Though his sydes gan to smerte.
>
> "Make glade chere," sayde Robyn Hode,
>   "Sheref, for charitë;
> For this is our ordre i-wys,
>   Under the grenë-wode tree."
>
> "This is harder order," sayde the sherief,
>   "Than any ankir or frere;

For all the golde in mery Englonde
I wolde not longe dwell here."

*   *   *   *   *

"Lat me go," than sayde the sherif,
   "For saynté charité,
And I wol be the besté frende
   That ever yet had ye."

So the sheriff swears a great oath never again to perse-
cute Robin and his men, and is suffered to go his way.
But he is false as water, and he breaks his pledge.   In
the end, however, after some stiff and joyous fighting,
he comes to grief.   In all these episodes the underlying motive, it will be perceived, is the injustice of
organized authority, as contrasted with the justice of
the greenwood.

It must be observed, on the other hand, that the outlaws themselves do not deal altogether fairly with the
sheriff.   From the modern point of view, Little John
is quite as treacherous as he.   At a contest in archery,
the wonderful shooting of Little John so arouses the
sheriff's admiration that he takes the yeoman, who
promptly gives a false name, into his service, bestowing
upon him a good horse and twenty marks a year.   But
Little John is no true servant.   He plunders the sheriff's
house, carrying away silver vessels and money, and
persuading one of the cooks in the kitchen to desert
his master.   All his booty he lays before Robin Hood,
and then betrays the sheriff into his hands.   Under
such circumstances, one cannot but feel some sympathy
with the unlucky official.   The relation between master
and man was in those days held to be peculiarly sacred,

and, in proving unfaithful, Little John was certainly guilty of dishonorable conduct. His justification in the ballads lies in the implication that he stands for the Right, and that the sheriff stands for the Wrong, and that in fighting evil anything is allowable. The Middle Ages believed firmly in the doctrine that the end justifies the means, and that no feelings of consideration or humanity need influence treatment of the wicked.

Very different from Robin's attitude towards the high sheriff of Nottingham is his behavior to the king. Obviously, he makes a sharp distinction between local and national authority. The power of the sheriff is to be flouted; the power of the ruler of all England is to be respected. When Robin sees the royal seal, he falls on his knees, and protests that he loves no man in the world so well as he does his sovereign. In the greenwood there are plenty of merry adventures in which the king takes part, but there is never any suggestion of a clash between the royal authority and the customs of the outlaws. There is none too much dignity about the monarch of the ballads; he seems to have little else to do than to indulge in woodland pranks, assuming the Lincoln green of the outlaws, and frightening the good people of Nottingham out of their wits, or going disguised into the forest, and joining in the woodland sports. He has something of the operatic sovereign about him. But the moment he is recognized, down go all the merry men on their knees. These ballads, then, are thoroughly patriotic. If they protest against abuses of Church and State, they nevertheless breathe allegiance to England. And the king, for his part, treats Robin Hood with distinguished consideration, —

the fact that he is a "proud outlaw" makes no difference.   Indeed, the term "outlaw" seems to be rather a
compliment than a reproach.   It does not mean what
we may hastily conclude that it means from modern
usage.   The leader of this forest company is an outlaw
only in that he refuses to recognize the authority of
unprincipled public servants; for the highest law in
the land, as embodied in the person of the king, he has
the deepest respect.

Robin Hood is one of those heroes whose fame rests
rather on a well-spent life than upon an heroic death.
He does not sacrifice everything in one supreme moment,
as Beowulf does when he meets the dragon, or as Roland
does in the pass of Roncesvalles.   His death is rather
an epilog than a chief action in the drama of his career.
It was necessary, however, to explain the disappearance
of so popular a figure, and so imagination has created a
circumstantial story of his last moments on earth, told
most fully in the ballad of 'Robin Hood's Death.'
The pleasant life in the greenwood has not protected
Robin from illness; he feels that no meat nor drink will
satisfy him until his veins have been opened, and some
of his blood has been let out, — the sovereign remedy
of the old days for many of the ills of the flesh.   His
kinswoman, the Prioress of Kirklees, will perform this
service for him, and so he takes leave of his merry men,
and, with no attendant but little John, goes off to seek
her.   But the Prioress is a wicked woman; she opens
his veins, and leaves him to bleed to death.   When he
is far spent, he faintly sounds his horn for help, like
Roland, and Little John comes in to soothe his dying
moments.   The details of this last scene differ; one

account adds a villain, "Red Roger," who thrusts him through the "milk-white side" as he lies all faint from loss of blood. Probably this was considered a more heroic end than the slow process of bleeding to death. There is a certain satisfaction in having the wounded hero make "dog's meat" of his assassin, with a mighty blow in the back. But Robin Hood will not grant the prayer of Little John, who proposes to burn the priory of Kirklees in revenge: —

"Now nay, now nay," quoth Robin Hood,
  "That boon I'll not grant thee;
I never hurt woman in all my life,
  Nor men in woman's company.

"I never hurt fair maid in all my time,
  Nor at mine end shall it be;
But give me my bent bow in my hand,
  And a broad arrow I'll let flee
And where this arrow is taken up,
  There shall my grave digged be.

"Lay me a green sod under my head,
  And another at my feet;
And lay my bent bow at my side,
  Which was my music sweet;
And make my grave of gravel and green,
  Which is most right and meet.

"Let me have length and breadth enough,
  With a green sod under my head,
That they may say, when I am dead,
  Here lies bold Robin Hood."

These words they readily granted him,
  Which did bold Robin please:
And there they buried bold Robin Hood,
  Within the fair Kirkleys.

In view of the whole tone and spirit of the Robin
Hood ballads, the almost complete absence of woman
and the love-element is hardly surprising. Women do
not belong in the rough outdoor life of the greenwood.
It is no place for homes and children, and the sturdy
morality of the English folk would tolerate no light
loves, no daughters of the regiment of easy virtue in
such a company as this. The reproach of unchastity is
reserved for the Prioress. We may be sure, too, that
the fact that Robin meets his death at the hands of a
member of the hated religious orders is not without
significance. Maid Marian, of course, does not belong in the good old Robin Hood tradition; she was
added to it in later times. Like Beowulf and Roland,
Robin Hood has weightier things to think about than
the love of woman. He holds them in all reverence,
but they make but little appeal to him. It is a survival of the old heroic spirit, which scorns to fall captive
to the softer emotions that enthrall the champions of
Romance. Gawain or Lancelot was easily won over
by a pretty face, — for them there lay more peril in a
lady's eyes than in twenty swords, indeed. But Robin
Hood is a prey to no such weakness. He has achieved
the community in which women have no part, dreamed
of by the King of Navarre in Shakspere's 'Love's
Labor's Lost,' and no Princess appears to show him the
folly of his ways.

We shall not be far wrong if we assign the ballads
which we have here been considering, those in which the
hero has a dignity and a simplicity unmarred by the
trivialities of later times, to the fourteenth century.
This was a period of unrest and confusion in Church

and State. The glory of the system of chivalry was passing; such a court as that of Edward the Third preserved a brave show, but its pageantry merely cloaked decay. The high ideals of the earlier conception of knighthood were observed rather in the letter than in the spirit. More than ever the upper classes were living for selfish and material ends; if they were forced to recognize the power of the common people as never before, they were none the less eager to press their own advantages to the utmost limits. Abuses of government, cruel and unjust taxation, which now and again met sturdy opposition, as in Wat Tyler's rebellion, were characteristic of the ruling powers of England. Not less selfish and corrupt than those were the clergy. The members of the great religious orders, which had done so much good on English soil, which had performed so many works of charity and devotion, were then too often grossly unfaithful to their vows of poverty, chastity, and obedience, and all the more blameworthy because they still maintained a pretence of allegiance to these vows. A multitude of unprincipled men went into the Church as an easy means of preying on the poor and simple. They accumulated vast wealth, while the commons starved and paid taxes.

These abuses, which had been steadily growing for a hundred years and more, were met at the end of the fourteenth century by a series of unusually vigorous protests, which were mirrored in various forms in contemporary literature. In the great poems attributed to a certain Langland, poems full of the most passionate indignation against social injustice, a mere plowman, the meanest in the social scale, is exalted above all

others. Passionate and indignant, too, were the utterances of even so gentle a man as the poet Gower.
Practical religious work and a seeking of the higher life,
rather than a struggle with the existing order of things,
marked the activity of Wicklif and his devoted followers. Chaucer was less filled with impulse to regenerate
the social order than to ridicule it; he indulged little
in passionate invective, but much in biting satire of
the hypocritical pretensions of the ecclesiastical orders.
Contrasted with all these is the spirit which created
Robin Hood, neither angry nor satirical, but good-
humored, gay, companionable, — tolerating, however,
no miscarriages of justice. The essential virtues of
the English commons, sturdy courage, robust morality,
and enthusiasm for fair play, are here crystallized
into a figure which contrasts sharply with the corruption of the nobles and ecclesiastics. Robin Hood was
not regarded as a robber, in the modern sense of the
term, he was a man who adjusted the inequalities of
wealth; he did not steal for personal aggrandizement,
but to assist the poor, and to punish those who amassed
wealth illegally. Moreover, Robin is no uncouth country fellow; the common people had progressed far
enough to desire him to have the virtues of the aristocracy, — elegant manners, for example. In the calm
strength and wisdom with which he acts, and the courtesy with which he accomplishes his ends, he rather
transcends what was possible for a yeoman of the fourteenth century.

It is most interesting to contrast this product of the
English folk with Reynard the Fox, a distinctively
French creation. Reynard is a gay fellow, but malicious

and evil-minded.   If he is merry, he snickers and leers.
There is many a broad horse-laugh in Robin's company,
but it is all honest mirth, with no sly deviltry about it.
Robin is devoted to religion; he is faithful to his king;
he is tender to women.   To Reynard all these things
are a mockery.   He sneers at religious observances,
parodying the offices of the Church with garbled ecclesiastical phrases; he pays no heed to the majesty of the
throne; he is callously cynical about the virtue of
women.   Most of all, however, he has no sense of fair
play; he is merely bent on doing as much mischief in the
world as he possibly can.   His grand mission in life is
to turn everything topsy-turvy, and then exult over the
confusion he has wrought.   The keynote of Robin's
efforts, on the other hand, is the preservation of justice.
By might he makes right, in an age in which impious
men bear sway.   He is bent on helping the world to be
better and happier, not to make everybody as uncomfortable as possible.   Reynard is an anarchist, of the
kind that tears down and thinks little of how to rebuild.
Robin is a socialist, but his program is as much con-
structive as destructive; he is quite as much bent on
helping the poor as in making things hot for rascals.
With his bluff and kindly nature, his love of the truth
and hatred of sham and oppression, he incarnates much
that is best in English character, — not wholly the
spirit of the Anglo-Saxon element, although this may be
held to predominate, but the spirit of the different
races which had combined to form the English people.

VIII

THE CANTERBURY TALES

O Socrates plains de philosophie,
Seneque en meurs et Anglux en pratique,
Ovides grans en ta poeterie,
Bries en parler, saiges en rethorique,
Aigles treshaulz, qui par ta theorique
Enluminez le regne d'Eneas,
L'Isle aux Geans, ceuls de Bruth, et qui as
Semé les fleurs et planté le rosier
Aux ignorans de la langue pandras.
Grant translateur, noble Geoffroy Chaucier.

— Eustache Deschamps.

VIII

THE CANTERBURY TALES

In the cartoons and caricatures which set forth current political events in our illustrated journals, we always recognize the United States in the familiar figure of Uncle Sam, a tall, raw-boned Yankee, with old-fashioned trousers and cowhide boots, and a swallowtail coat made of the Stars and Stripes. We look upon him, of course, only as a symbol; we know that if the distinctive characteristics of the American people were ever represented by such a personage as this, they can no longer be so represented at the present day. Uncle Sam is no more like the average American than the pot-bellied choleric John Bull of the cartoonists is like the average Englishman. And when we consider the matter further, we realize how impossible it is to represent the typical American by any one figure. Our country is too complex for such simplification, — a thousand types cannot well be rolled into one. Even if the field be narrowed to New York City alone, the problem becomes no easier. There is perhaps as much racial and temperamental diversity in this one municipality as in all the rest of the United States together. The elements which compose such a community are too manifold and too varied ever to be reduced to a single adequate and comprehensive symbol,

197

even though the cartoonist has created a Father Knickerbocker, emblematic of early New Amsterdam rather than of later New York.

If this is true of America at the present day, it was also true of England in the fourteenth century, and if it is true of modern New York, it was almost as true of medieval London. In the days of Chaucer, the various professions and trades were sharply differentiated, and distinctions of rank and station were strongly marked. The complex society of that age formed a striking contrast to the society which produced 'Beowulf,' or the 'Song of Roland.' The Anglo-Saxon community had been much simpler; there had been fewer differences of rank and of occupation, men had thought and felt more as a group and less as a collection of individuals. The same statement applies, with some modifications, to the French at the time of the Conquest. The 'Song of Roland' is the epic of a folk still mainly homogeneous. But as we approach modern times, the social order grows steadily more complicated, and in the Arthurian romances, in the story of Reynard the Fox, and in the ballads of Robin Hood, we have to deal not with the literature of the nation as a whole, but with that of separate groups and classes. Now, at the close of our survey of the social tendencies of the English people in early times, we may well endeavor to gain a bird's-eye view of all these contrasting types, to look at them not by themselves, but as parts of a great whole.

There can be no better way to gain this bird's-eye view than to make the pilgrimage to Canterbury with the nine and twenty English men and women to whom Chaucer has introduced us in his 'Canterbury Tales.'

Here almost every walk of life is represented, but a
certain unity is given to the expedition, not only because
these travelers are all English, but because they are
animated by the same purpose, — they are all on their
way to the same shrine.   In the fourteenth century
the trip from London to Canterbury consumed three
or four days, but this delay may not have been without its compensations.   It must have been delightful
to ride in the springtime on horseback through the leafy
English lanes, and along the highroad with the green
fields on either hand.   It was safer as well as pleasanter
to travel with others, since thieves were plentiful and
the roads none too well guarded.   Chaucer, who rides
in the company himself, could tell you, if he chose, of
the dangers of traveling alone with money in your
purse, for he has more than once been robbed of considerable sums, while in the king's service.   And no
member of the company takes more pleasure in the
good-fellowship of the expedition than this shy man,
who has revealed to us the characteristics of his countrymen with such unfailing humor and genial sympathy.

The avowed object of our expedition is to offer
prayers at the shrine of St. Thomas of Canterbury, the
great English martyr, whose tomb has now become a
spot of especial sanctity.   Many of the party are doubtless fulfilling some vow made in the course of the past
year; it is a common practice to promise the saint the
honor of a pilgrimage to his shrine in return for his protection.   Others are ecclesiastics, whose profession
makes an occasional journey such as this a matter of
duty.   The purpose of each man and woman is, no
doubt, avowedly religious.   But, after all, the real

reason why most of them are undertaking this pilgrimage to Canterbury is quite different, — they want a little spring holiday. They are seeking amusement and relaxation, they look forward with keen anticipation to the pleasure of riding through the sweet country, all fresh with green leaves and bright flowers after the April rains; they like to gossip and chat with their fellow-travelers, and they will find much to interest them later on in the bustling little town of Canterbury. Any place which shelters the shrine of a popular saint is sure to be thriving. This pilgrimage is, in short, a summer vacation for all these people, and it is all the more satisfying, since they can do something to save their souls and enjoy themselves at the same time, — not always a possible combination! One of the company, a stout and rather masculine widow from the town of Bath, who has made a snug fortune in cloth-weaving, is exceedingly fond of travel, and has been all over Europe on pilgrimages of this sort. She has visited many foreign shrines, that of St. James of Campostella in Spain, and that of the Virgin in Boulogne just across the Channel. She has been to Cologne, where lie the bones of the three Wise Men of the East, and she has even ventured as far as Rome. When made by land, these have not been difficult journeys; the roads, smoothed by the passing of thousands of pilgrims, are suitably provided with inns, where travelers are refreshed and sheltered; there are guide-books telling the proper way to take, — in short, everything possible is done for the convenience and comfort of wayfarers. Whether one prefers a Continental tour, or merely a little excursion in the English country, the pilgrim routes will offer, in this reign of King Richard the Second, the safest and pleasantest opportunity to see a little of the world.

At a comfortable inn, the Tabard in Southwark, our travelers have just been resting before beginning the actual journey to Canterbury. Their accommodations at this hostelry are satisfactory; the rooms are large, the stables are capacious, and the host is personally attentive to their wants. He is a merry and good-natured man, fond of his joke, but nevertheless with an eye to the main chance. The hotel business has been good, and he feels that he can afford to take a little vacation, and ride down to Canterbury himself, but he reflects that it would be a good stroke of policy to gather all this party into his house on the way back. So at supper-time, when all are feeling in good humor, he proposes that for diversion by the wayside each shall entertain the rest of the company by story-telling, and that the man who tells the best tale of all shall be given a dinner at the expense of the others when they return to London. And the host is very particular to have it clearly understood that this dinner must be in his own hotel, "here in this place, sitting by this post," as he says. He himself offers to act as guide on the way, and to serve as judge and presiding officer when the story-telling goes on. To this plan the travelers gladly assent, the wine is once more brought in, and everybody goes to bed. In the morning, the host bustles about like a cock among a flock of hens, routing out those who are sleeping late after the potations of the evening before, and, in his capacity as manager of the expedition, seeing to it that an early start is made for Canterbury. As soon as all have gone a little distance on the way, he calls for the first tale, and the game is fairly begun.

We are fortunate in having, in this company, representatives of nearly all ranks of English society. There are persons of nobility, a knight and his son, an esquire, who are given a certain precedence over the rest. The knight is a distinguished man, who has seen much service in Continental wars, and who shows his breeding in his modesty and in his consideration for those about him. His son, dressed in the height of fashion, fancies himself so deep in love that he can hardly get any sleep at night, and spends his days in singing sentimental songs. We have seen lovers of this type before, in the romances. There is also a prioress, a lady of gentle blood who has taken religious vows. She shows her superior social position in her elegant table manners, — she is careful not to wet her fingers in the gravy, and when she drinks out of the cup as it goes around the table, she leaves it clean for the next person who uses it. Other pilgrims represent the well-to-do upper middle class, and some of them even make pretensions to superior gentility. Our friend the widow of Bath, who has buried five husbands, and gone all over Europe seeking consolation, is a person of some wealth and consequence, and is disposed to insist that others shall recognize this. If any one ventures to precede her in church on a Sunday, when she is awfully arrayed in a voluminous headdress, she loses her temper completely, and that is no small matter. There is also a country gentleman or franklin, who has held various public offices, and aspires to be thought aristocratic. While at home he always keeps open house in magnificent style, and his manners on this journey savor of the pride that apes humility.

There are many ecclesiastics in the party, from the fat and overfed monk, who spends most of his time in hunting, and who gives more thought to dress than to religion, down to the poor parish priest, who labors in a straggling country district, where he must walk on foot from house to house on his errands of mercy and cheer. This rural parson is almost the only man of the group of churchmen who is not a rascal. They are not, as a whole, a pleasant set of people. There is a waggish fellow who makes a living by traveling about through the country districts selling bogus relics, — pigs' bones, which he tries to pass off as those of the saints, and an old pillow-case which he avers is a part of the veil of the Blessed Virgin. He also peddles indulgences, which give the buyer the right to sin without offending the Church. There is a begging friar, too, who is little better than an impostor, wheedling the rich and squeezing the poor. But he has the saving grace of being able to play on the harp and fiddle, and after he has finished his songs, his eyes twinkle in his head like the stars on a frosty night! He is not so bad a companion, though scarcely to be respected. Far less agreeable is the summoner, a ribald fellow of unclean life, whose duty it is to act as a police officer for the Bishop's court, and bring up to justice those who are guilty of spiritual offenses. He is feared and hated, because he uses his power to extort money unlawfully. We must not forget the priests in attendance upon the lady prioress, who is a person of such consequence that she must go well escorted. They are not particularly described, so we may give them the benefit of the doubt, and set them down as honest men. We can hardly think ill of the priest who tells the pretty story of the cock and the fox, at all events. But most of the pilgrims who represent the Church do not inspire confidence.

There are respectable solid tradesmen, members of the great English guilds, or trades-unions, and there is a yeoman, who looks as though he might have come straight from the merry band of Robin Hood in Sherwood forest, with his coat and hood of green, and his bow and peacock-feathered arrows. There is a doctor and a lawyer and a student at Oxford University, — we cannot stay to describe them all. Chaucer is particularly amused at the shrewdness of the steward or manciple, who purchases provisions for the Inns of Court, — a rascal who can deceive the keenest lawyers, and well line his pockets with money stolen from his patrons. "Doesn't it show the grace of God," Chaucer slyly asks, "that the wit of such an ignorant fellow should surpass the wisdom of a heap of learned men?"

Finally, we must observe certain members of the company at whom the dainty prioress and the purse-proud gentleman farmer look a little askance, — uncouth fellows from the lower walks of life, who betray their grossness in their ribald speech. There is a cook named Roger who is drunk most of the time, so that he even falls from his horse and has to be helped out of the mire. Yet he is a man who can bake a pie in a masterly fashion, although the host insinuates that he sometimes uses flies when parsley is not at hand. There is a sailor, too, who rides his horse as awkwardly as the drunken cook, a man who has seen rough service, and made his enemies walk the plank on the high seas. Another stout fellow is a miller, not over honest in his trade, and full of loud talk and coarse jests. The pilgrims ride out of town to the skirling of his bagpipes, while the pardoner and the summoner join from time to time in a duet — "Come hither, love, to me!" and the friar and the young esquire contribute their share, vocally and instrumentally, to the entertainment of their fellows and to the easement of their own hearts. Truly, there is music and to spare on this jolly pilgrimage, and some of the greatest rascals have the merriest notes.

The host does his part in admirable fashion, keeping order, quieting the disagreements which occasionally arise, bringing forward the shyer spirits and repressing the more forward ones when he can. Some of the ruder knaves are so anxious to have their say that they actually obtain precedence over the gentlefolk. We cannot be absolutely sure of the sequence of the tales, but we can see clearly enough that it is not determined by the rank of the tellers. The young esquire, for example, has to wait until after the miller and the cook and the sailor and others of their class have finished. The host is shrewd enough to see to it in the very beginning that the knight, the most distinguished man in the whole company, shall tell the first tale. Although the host pretends to arrange the matter by drawing lots, we know well enough that he manages so that the game shall be properly begun. After this he allows the others to follow almost at random. He tells no story himself, but he expresses his opinions freely from time to time.

He does not interfere with the most ribald of jests;
he likes a good racy tale himself, and he knows that
even the more refined members of the company will
relish coarse talk too. The elegant young esquire is,
upon occasion, as gross as any one. It is an era of
license in speech and jest. At the same time, the host
is equally generous to dullness. Men of the Middle
Ages seem to have felt that the most unbearably tedious
moralizing is a good thing for the soul, as bitter herbs
are best for the digestion. Only once is the host obliged
to interrupt a speaker in the midst of his tale ; when
Chaucer is mouthing an absurd parody on the grandilo-
quent romances of the day, the heroics of chivalry reduced to farce, and makes his adventurous knight drink
nothing but water, — then the host's patience is ex-
hausted. Where would be the profits of the good ale
of the Tabard Inn if every one were to become a teeto-
taler? It is monstrous to think of, not a matter to
be touched upon even in jest.

This pilgrimage is a kind of open forum, in which
every one speaks his mind, and gives his views on a
variety of subjects under color of story-telling. These
people debate as well as narrate, as various questions
arise — social, moral, religious, and literary — which
claim their interest. And these debates are carried on
most informally; every one has a right to be heard,
the commons as well as the gentlefolk. A thoroughly
democratic spirit prevails. This is one of the most
striking things about the 'Canterbury Tales,' that here,
for the first time in English literature, all classes meet in
mutual sympathy and fellowship on a common footing
as human beings. Does not this mark the beginning

of a better social consciousness than has hitherto existed, does it not indicate in some degree a breaking of the barriers of caste? Launcelot would not have condescended to travel with a plowman or a cook, — when he once had to ride in a cart he felt it a gross indignity, quite beneath what was proper for one of his rank. It seems doubtful whether Gawain, with all his vaunted courtesy, would have liked the free and easy humors of the Canterbury pilgrimage much better. In this company, however, the persons of superior social station are not haughty. The knight is as modest as a maiden; never in his life has he been discourteous to any one. The squire does not hesitate to bandy a coarse jest about the table, and the much-traveled widow, the wife of Bath, although she may put on some airs in church, is the best of company, laughing and talking in a spirit of complete good-fellowship. When the gentleman farmer, who is really the only snob in the party, regrets that his son had rather talk with a servant than with a person of higher rank, the host rudely retorts, "A straw for thy 'gentility'!" The host is, indeed, an embodiment of the common sympathy which exists between the different members of the company. His utterances as presiding officer are truly representative of the body which he governs, so that when he is respectful to the poor parson, but waggish with the more important churchmen, he is merely voicing the sentiments of the party as a whole.

Despite this democratic spirit, no effort is made by the various pilgrims to adapt their tales to the taste of the company as a whole. On the contrary, each offers a story of the kind which he has been accustomed to hear, addressing himself to those of the party who care for the same sort of entertainment as he does himself. The coarser natures do not derive much satisfaction from the delicate narratives of their betters, and no effort is made to add salt to those narratives for their benefit. On the other hand, the good parson and the lady prioress can hardly have approved of the lewd yarns of the miller or the sailor; but these worthies bate no jot of their rough fun to save the feelings of more squeamish souls. There is rarely any hint of insincerity among the pilgrims; they are frank and un-abashed at all times. What they have to say is thoroughly characteristic of their breeding and their tastes. Thus their tales afford a comprehensive view of the principal types of medieval narrative, as developed by the different classes of society; they illustrate vividly the aristocratic and democratic tendencies in the life of the times.

We have already traced these contrasting tendencies in the romances of King Arthur and his knights, and in the verse dealing with Reynard the Fox and with Robin Hood. We have noted that the aristocracy loved un-real, fantastic narratives, exalting the courage and courtesy of some romantic hero, and his undying love for a fair lady. Such stories we have here, told, as one might expect, by the knight and his son, and by the wife of Bath and the country gentleman. Very typical is the tale of the wife of Bath, full of the absurdities of romance, and yet touched with its evanescent charm and illumined by its Quixotic ideality. After a long and most entertaining account of the management of her five husbands, the good lady finally comes to her story. The hero is a knight of King Arthur's court, who has been condemned to death for a grievous fault. At the last moment Queen Guinevere takes pity on him, and begs the king to spare his life. Her prayer is granted, but the queen tells the unhappy knight that there is one more condition which he must fulfil before he can be a free man; he must be able to give the right answer to this question: "What do women most desire?" This task seems to the knight indeed difficult, but he goes forth, resolved to discover the true answer if he can. So he asks every one whom he meets. Some people tell him that women love riches, others say that they desire honor most of all, others pleasure, others dress, others flattery, but none of these solutions seems quite satisfactory. One day, as the knight is out in the forest, he comes upon a hideously ugly old woman, to whom he tells his trouble. She promises to give him the right answer, if he will grant her one favor in return. This the knight readily promises, and she tells him the secret. Then they go up to the court together, and there, before the whole multitude surrounding the king and queen, the knight delivers the answer, — the dearest thing to the heart of a woman is power, domination. "My liege lady," he says, addressing the queen, "women in general desire to have sovereignty over their husbands and their lovers, and to have their own way about everything." All agree that this is the right answer, and the knight is pardoned. Suddenly, up starts the hideous old woman, and demands her reward. This is — that the knight shall marry her! But now observe the reward of courtesy. The knight is so perfect a gentleman that he not only makes her his wife, but allows her what she has said women most desire, — to have her own way in everything. As soon as she has obtained his consent to this arrangement, she is suddenly transformed into a beautiful young woman. She has been bewitched, doomed to ugliness until she can find a man willing to marry her, and subject himself completely to her will.

This fantastic story, probably ultimately derived from the treasure-house of Celtic narrative, is an excellent illustration of the conventions of chivalry, according to which a knight must obey the will of his lady, and must be courteous and self-sacrificing in all things, no matter how great a strain may be put upon his patience. Originally a widespread folk-tale, it was so well suited to the taste of the upper classes that it was made peculiarly their own. It was frequently told of Sir Gawain, the model of medieval courtesy. Here it is narrated quite seriously until the end, when the wife of Bath exaggerates the moral so that the story becomes truly absurd. "And so," she says, "the knight and his lady live until the end of their lives in perfect joy. And may Christ send us young and meek husbands, and grant that we may outlive them! And I also pray the Lord that He will shorten the lives of all those who will not be governed by their wives! And old and angry niggards, who won't spend their money, — may God send to them a very pestilence!" All this is good-humored fun, yet there is a meaning beneath it. When the wife of Bath tells this courtly tale, with its setting in the domains of King Arthur, as an illustration of her advanced views about the way to treat husbands, and when she makes the chivalrous deference of a gentle-

man to the will of his lady mean complete extinction
of his personality, she deals a heavy blow to the conventions of aristocratic literature. If the tale were not
in itself absurd, from the point of view of common-
sense, it would not form so delicious a defense of her
humorous thesis. Beneath the mask of the wife of
Bath Chaucer is here having a little fling at the weak-
nesses of the system of chivalry, just as in the 'Rime
of Sir Topaz' he parodies the ludicrous bombast of the
metrical romances, or as he occasionally puts his tongue
in his cheek while the knight is telling his elaborately
artificial tale. The aristocratic conventions which we
have seen in all their glory in the Arthurian romances
were already on the decline in Chaucer's day. They
had done their service, in helping to refine the taste of
a brutal age. But now this service was no longer so
much appreciated; their absurdity was sometimes more
apparent than their idealism.

The tales of the common folk contain many a caustic
comment on the aristocratic manners of the day. We
have already seen two separate tendencies in the literature of the middle classes, — the one satirical, mocking
with bitter laughter at Church and State through the
mouth of Reynard the Fox; the other a more digni-
fied and good-humored protest uttered by Robin Hood.
In the 'Canterbury Tales' the bitter and cynical tone
is very noticeable in the criticism of life which comes
from the commons. These folk have sharp tongues;
they love to ridicule the errors of churchmen and the
frailties of women. Chivalry had insisted on blind
devotion to the gentler sex and to the majesty of religion; these people answer, with a sneer, that neither

women nor clerics are any better than they should be.
Most of their stories will not bear repeating. The
closest modern analogues of these *fabliaux*, told among
men in the ale-house and tavern, are our smoking-room
stories, indefensibly coarse, even though indisputably
humorous. The grossness of Chaucer's tales is well-
known, but they have some redeeming qualities. They
differ from their descendants of the smoking-room in
that they are really artistic in their narrative method,
the precursors of the modern short-story, and that they
contain, under their broad jesting, mordant social satire.
The knight tells a tale of two lovesick young warriors,
Palamon and Arcite, who woo a pink and white beauty
named Emily with all the elaborate mannerisms of
romance. Hardly has the knight finished, when the
drunken miller steps in and shows what the common
people made of the airs and graces of aristocracy. His
heroes are two rascally young " clerks "; his heroine
a carpenter's wife of doubtful virtue. The extravagant
way in which these two knaves make love to the lady
is no less than a parody of the sentimentality of the
knight's tale. One of them sings love-songs and sighs
under her window: —

> The mone, whan it was night, ful brighte shoon,
> And Absolon his giterne hath y-take,
> For paramours, he thoughte for to wake.[1]
> And forth he gooth, Iolif and amorous,
> Til he cam to the carpenteres hous
> A little after cokkes hadde y-crowe;
> And dressed hym up by a shot-windowe
> That was upon the carpenteres wal.
> He singeth in his vois gentil and smal,

[1] " For love-longing, he had no thought of sleeping."

"Now, dere lady, if thy wille be,
I preye yow that ye wol rewe on me,"
Ful wel acordaunt to his giterninge.

This is the final outcome of the absurdities of the system of chivalry in the minds of the sharp-witted common folk; caricature of its elaborate manners, and
satire of its immorality, which permitted a married
woman to encourage the love of other men than her
husband.

We must be careful not to take all that is said in
the 'Canterbury Tales' about the faults and failings of
women too seriously. It represents truly neither
Chaucer's feelings nor those of his age. The frailty
of women formed one of the stock subjects for medieval
satire, just as her peerless perfection served as the
corner-stone of the system of chivalry. Both of these
artificial literary fashions affect the spontaneity of the
sentiments of the pilgrims. Again, some other tales,
like that of the lawyer, are not intended to be taken
seriously at all; they exaggerate the virtue of woman
out of all reason for a moral purpose. The young
Oxford student tells of the patient Griselda, who was
so obedient to her husband that she was willing to let
him kill her children and put her aside for another
wife, and yet make no complaint. This represents the
ideals of no class of society; Chaucer himself says that
the tale is not told because wives ought to imitate the
humility of Griselda, for that would be unbearable,
even if they were willing to try, but because every one
ought to be constant in adversity, as she was. We may
fancy the disgust of the wife of Bath at this story!
And then, by way of antidote, Chaucer tells of the

lean cow which fed on patient wives, and the fat cow
which fed on patient husbands, showing, just as in the
wife of Bath's tale, that the moral must be taken with
a grain of salt. We must surely disregard such evidence as this in studying Chaucer's work as an indication of social ideals. It is the expression of individuals, it smells of the lamp, it is little connected with
that literature which rises spontaneously from the
thoughts and feelings of any great class of society; or,
if it was once the property of the people, it has been
so altered in learned hands as to be completely changed
in spirit. The 'Canterbury Tales,' it will be observed,
are not like the great poetry which we have considered
in the earlier lectures, — they are a collection of diverse
material, some of it popular, some of it aristocratic,
some of it learned and "literary." In so far as these
stories mark the emergence of the individual, or the
narrow interests of the moralist, they are a less trustworthy guide to social progress.

Yet this very diversity is itself significant. We have
now, at the end of the fourteenth century, reached a
time when story-telling no longer reflects the ideals of
a few sharply defined social orders, but when it is complicated in a thousand ways by the more elaborate
structure of the English nation. It is more difficult
to see English life clearly because it is no longer simple. Its confusion appeared so great to the author of
"Piers Plowman" — if we may speak of him as one man
— that he represented it as a field full of folk of the
most diverse habits and occupations, a motley throng
indeed. Despite his vivid characterizations, he did
not succeed in interpreting the true spirit of the time

as Chaucer did. Chaucer's vision is wider; he sees virtue in many classes of society, while Langland is so intent on remedying social abuses that he has little sympathy for any one but his plowman hero. Langland shows us many vividly contrasted types, but Chaucer introduces us more intimately to the people themselves. He makes them speak, sometimes formally, when they are entertaining the rest of the pilgrims, sometimes informally, but always naturally. What any group of persons say is quite as important for an understanding of their true character as how they look. There is no one figure in the Field of Folk so complex and at the same time so human as the wife of Bath, but if Chaucer had contented himself with mere description, her personality would have been far less vivid. The same is true of many of the other characters. And Chaucer had a sympathetic understanding of them all. It is indeed rare in any age to find an author with interests so wide as to embrace all classes of people, acquainted with all kinds of story-telling, from saints' lives to the coarse jests of the tavern, and with the power to put before us a human comedy perfectly representative of his age, making his men and women reveal, by means of narratives told by themselves, their own thoughts and ideals.

For such a task as this Chaucer was particularly fitted by his experience with all sorts and conditions of men. He lived in London, then, as now, the heart of England. He was born a commoner, but he spent his earlier years at the royal court. He was thrown on terms of intimacy with the greatest in the land, he was an active man of business, he was a traveler in foreign countries, he was a soldier who saw active service in the field, he was a member of Parliament, and the holder of various public offices, and he was a diplomatist, engaged in important and confidential negotiations. His career was far more varied than Shakspere's, it will be observed. Shakspere was, indeed, a shrewd man of business, he lived in London in a most picturesque and active era, and he was on intimate terms with persons of distinguished birth and superior breeding. But that he was ever more than an actor and a sharer in theatrical enterprises there is nothing to show. His life was passed in the midst of most interesting scenes, but he took only a restricted share in the manifold activities of his day. He was able to devote his full energies to the drama, while with Chaucer literary work was of necessity subordinated to business. Shakspere passed the best years of his life in the atmosphere of the theater; Chaucer was constantly obliged to give up his books and his writing in order to discharge faithfully the duties which had been laid upon him. Charles Lamb used to assert that his real "works" were in the rolls of the East India Office; Chaucer might have said that his own were in the ledgers of the Customs Office for the Port of London. For a considerable time he was obliged to fill in these ledgers with entries in his own handwriting. In this work many hours were consumed which might have given classics to the world. His public occupations claimed so much of his time through the prime of his life that it seems a marvel that he produced as much as he did. But all this activity among many classes of men, in swarming London, in Italy in the springtime of the Renaissance, in France and in Flanders, gave him the breadth of view, the insight into human nature, the poise of judgment, which make his work so perfect a mirror of his own day. Had he spent more time among his books, and less in the great world, he might have been less representative of his age. The imprisonment of his gay spirit behind the bars of routine may perhaps have even given his song an added freshness when once the doors of his cage were opened.

He viewed the human comedy with a certain detachment. As a man of the world, he was interested in a great variety of things, but, like Horace, without the deepest feeling. He never quite lets himself go; if he becomes tragic or tender, he is likely to turn aside with a shrug and a smile, and to deny his own emotion. He identifies himself with no one class of society; he stands apart, and views them all from his own point of vantage. When he exposes the abuses of the times, he is rather amused than indignant. If monks and friars steal from the poor, and meanwhile line their own pockets, he has more real delight in seeing through their hypocritical pretenses than he has righteous anger at their villainy. Nothing pleases him more than to set two of them against each other, to make the summoner and the friar expose each other's tricks. He is no particular friend of the commons. He hates shams and hypocrisies, in whatever station. The miller who steals corn, or the sailor who is sometimes dishonest and cruel, are treated with as little mercy as the lawyer or the doctor. Chaucer does not lift up his voice in favor of the lower classes, like Langland or Gower. In fact he seems, like Shakspere, to have been rather impatient of the multi-

tude.   He is no brother of the men who gave final form
to the stories of Reynard the Fox.   Probably he had
seen enough of the turbulent commons of his day to
despise their instability and treachery.   "O stormy
people," he exclaims, "so little serious, so little true to
what you say!   Ever indiscreet, changing like a
weathercock, delighting in rumor, waxing and waning
like the moon, full of gabble, your judgments are false,
your constancy is vain, the man who believes in you
is a great fool!"   This is what differentiates Chaucer
from many other great literary men of his day.   He
had no desire to reform the world; he merely strove
to show it as it was.   His attitude was akin to that of
Shakspere and of Molière.   We have long since aban-
doned the absurd notion that a definite didactic purpose was the controlling force in the composition of the
plays of Shakspere.   We know, too, that while Molière
doubtless produced 'Tartuffe' partly in order to strike
at hypocrisy, and 'L'Avare' partly to expose avarice,
his genius was not confined with limits so narrow;
his ultimate object was not to fulfil the functions of a
Bossuet or of a La Rochefoucauld, but to show life in
the large as he saw it in the brilliant and varied society
of his day.

On the other hand, the personality of the author is
far more in evidence in the work of Chaucer than in
the plays of these great dramatists.   In this respect,
Chaucer is more like Thackeray, who constantly interrupts his narrative in order to interject remarks in
his own person.   Chaucer rides with his pilgrims, he
is one of their company, he tells two of the stories himself.   But he is not content to appear merely as a char-

acter, he speaks out as author too. Sometimes he gets so much interested in his tale that he forgets that one of his characters is telling it. Suddenly the mask drops, and it is Chaucer who addresses us straight from the desk where he is writing, and not even from his place in the procession on the road to Canterbury. It is surely not the shy and serious Oxford student who finishes the tale of the patient Griselda. At the end of the story, after the irritating patience of the virtuous wife has been finally rewarded, a half-waggish, half-cynical epilog follows, at which we have already glanced. Every reader must feel that the clerk of Oxford has faded out of the picture completely, and that Chaucer has usurped his place. Rightly enough the scribe has written above the lines, "L'Envoy de Chaucer."

Griselda is dead, and her patience too! And I warn all married men not to try the patience of their wives in the hopes of finding a Griselda, for they'll surely fail! . . . Stand at your defense, ye arch-wives, I counsel you! Since you are as strong as camels, don't suffer men to offend you! And ye slender wives, feeble in fighting, be savage as Indian tigers, keep on gabbling as fast as a mill, I counsel you! . . . Make your husbands jealous, and you shall make them couch like quails. . . . Be light as leaf on linden tree, and let your husbands have sorrow and weeping, wailing and wringing of hands!

Chaucer was not, of course, the originator of his tales; he borrowed them from whatever sources he chose, and in many cases these sources were truly popular — as much so as those of the Robin Hood ballads or of the stories of Reynard the Fox. But in placing them in a distinctive and picturesque framework, in which he himself appeared, Chaucer emphasized the personal note almost as much as he did by his comments delivered in his capacity as author. His great contemporary and master in story-telling, Boccaccio, does not appear among the noble company in the 'Decameron,' nor does he express his own ideas about their conduct. Chaucer's friend and fellow-townsman, Gower, speaks in his own person in his collection of tales, the 'Confessio Amantis,' but only as a sort of lay-figure, conversing with an impossible half-mythological, half-allegorical figure, the Priest of Venus. But Chaucer moves among the pilgrims a live and breathing man, full of spirit and humor. He was medieval in his willingness to tell absurd and archaic stories, full of the artificial conventions of chivalry or the exaggerations of morality and religion common to his day, but he was modern in his fresh and common-sense outlook upon life, and in his willingness to let this influence his work. Even when he is not speaking, we constantly feel his presence. He takes us into his confidence; he draws us aside and laughs with us at the merry jest of life. By a supreme stroke of genius, he reveals to us a personality more fascinating and more complex than that of any of his pilgrims, — his own.

We cannot delay over an analysis of his genius; our main emphasis must be on his stories and their significance for the social conditions of his age. But this may be said ere we take leave of him: he was as great a poet as a man can be who rarely achieves pathos and who never attains sublimity.

We have now reached the close of the Middle Ages, and in the era of Chaucer, stand on the threshold of modern times. The Reformation and the Renaissance are to bring new tendencies, foreign to the characteristic habits of medieval thought. New interests excite the minds of men; their whole angle of vision changes. The old fashions in literature have not lost their potency, of course; the machinery of chivalry is destined to survive in poetry, as in society, long after its true glory has departed. But it will be merely as a survival, no longer with the freshness of youth and vigor upon it. The mouthings of Hawes' 'Pastime of Pleasure' weary us, naturally, but even so noble a piece of prose as the 'Morte Darthur' or so great a poem as Spenser's 'Faery Queene' are really archaisms, divorced from intimate connection with the times in which they were produced. Literary periods are hard to determine, but with Chaucer we may well take leave of a definite epoch, and turn the leaf to a new chapter of history. Our present task is now completed; before leaving it we may take one glance behind over what we have done.

We have followed from the beginnings the social and political progress of the English people, beginning with 'Beowulf,' which reveals a people democratic in instinct, though aristocratic in political organization, — a people whose hearts were chiefly set on war, who felt far less the calls of religion and of patriotism. In the 'Song of Roland' we have seen how the incoming French brought with them new ideals of the Christian faith and of the love of country. We have seen, too, how the Celtic peoples, so long repressed by the later conquerors of Britain, came into their own at last by impressing their ideality upon the France of a later day, and by aiding to create that finer code of manners and morals which we call chivalry. We have seen the worldly side of this movement exemplified in Arthur, Launcelot, Gawain, and

Tristram; the religious side in the legends of the Holy Grail. The gap between the upper and lower classes of society is widest at this point; in the Arthurian legends the aristocracy and the commons are far apart indeed. But in the democratic protests of Reynard the Fox and of Robin Hood the people asserted their rights. At the end of the fourteenth century, these two tendencies, the aristocratic and the democratic, were no longer pursuing independent lines of development. There was an end to stolid acceptance of the existing order of things by the peasantry, and to the supreme indifference of the ruling classes to interests other than their own. It was no longer possible for each to go its own way. In spite of great political unrest, of grave economic and religious disorders, there was now a social consciousness which had not hitherto existed. Of this the 'Canterbury Tales' are the literary embodiment. It was not, however, a time of final adjustment; it was an era of change and of confusion. Nor were the years immediately following to bring harmony. The Wars of the Roses were not far away; greater religious troubles than Lollardry were on the horizon; worse monarchs than Richard the Second were to sit on the throne of England. But this very restlessness and change was itself a sign of new independence of thought and new initiative to action. The principle of the modern English constitution that the people as a whole shall govern was making itself felt in good earnest; the struggles of modern times were just beginning. With these later struggles, at which we have glanced in the opening lecture, we are not here concerned. But we shall understand better their complications when we remember the characteristics of the races which went to the making of the English people, their several contributions to its temper and spirit, and the changing ideals of heroism, patriotism, religion, and courtesy, so vividly revealed in their heroic and romantic stories, ideals from which has sprung the finer social consciousness of modern times.

APPENDIX

SUGGESTIONS FOR SUPPLEMENTARY READING

(The bibliographical references here given aim merely to suggest some of the more helpful editions, translations, and critical discussions. A more detailed bibliography will be found in one or more of the works cited under each subject-heading.)

I. General Introduction. W. P. Ker's *Epic and Romance* (Macmillan, 1908) forms a delightful survey of the principal types of medieval literature. A review of the development of European literature as a whole is afforded by the series edited by Saintsbury (Scribner's, 1904, etc.) : *The Dark Ages*, by W. P. Ker ; *The Flourishing of Romance and the Rise of Allegory*, by G. Saintsbury ; *The Fourteenth Century*, by F. J. Snell ; *The Transition Period*, by G. Gregory Smith. For a compact and comprehensive review of French literature see G. Paris, *La littérature française au moyen âge* (3d ed., Paris, Hachette, 1905) ; or *Medieval French Literature* (London, Dent, 1903) in the *Temple Primers Series*. For conditions in England in the later period see W. H. Schofield, *English Literature from the Norman Conquest to Chaucer* (Macmillan, 1906). Other excellent surveys of these fields are Petit de Julleville, *Histoire de la langue et de la littérature française*, — contributions by various scholars — Vols. I and II (Paris, Colin, 1896) ; J. Bédier and P. Hazard, *Histoire de la littérature française*, 2 vols. (Paris, Larousse) ; and *The Cambridge History of English Literature*, Vols. I and II (Putnam, 1907, 1908). A study of medieval literature should be supplemented by the use of a good outline of historical conditions, such as J. H. Robinson's *Introduction to the History of Western Europe*, revised edition (Ginn, 1924), or Lynn Thorndike's *Medieval Europe* (London, Harrap, 1920). G. B. Adams'

Civilization during the Middle Ages (N. Y., 1898) will be found very suggestive. Especial mention should be made of Professor W. M. Hart's *Ballad and Epic; a Study in the Development of the Narrative Art,* in *Harvard Studies and Notes,* Vol. XI (Ginn, 1907). For the social development of the English people the reader may consult the large work by H. D. Traill, *Social England,* 6 vols. (N. Y., 1893–1897). Henry Osborn Taylor's *The Medieval M nd,* 2 vols. (Macmillan, third American edition, 1919), which reviews important aspects of medieval literature, may be strongly recommended.

II. Beowulf. Translated into alliterative verse by F. B. Gummere, *The Oldest English Epic* (Macmillan, 1909), with excellent introduction and notes, and with other pieces of Anglo-Saxon heroic verse included. Another verse-rendering is that by J. Lesslie Hall (Heath, 1901). Of prose versions, that by J. R. Clark Hall (London, Sonnenschein, 1901) has considerable supplementary material, and is so arranged as to bring out the main events of the poem distinctly; those by Child (*Riverside Literature Series,* Houghton, Mifflin) and C. B. Tinker (N. Y., Newson, 1905) are inexpensive and reliable. These translations will be found to vary considerably in their interpretation of specific passages. The best discussion of the many vexed questions relating to the origins and development of the poem is R. W. Chambers's *Introduction to the Study of Beowulf* (Cambridge, Eng., 1921). Analyses in encyclopedias and handbooks should be taken with great caution. The student may be referred to the brief introduction to Gummere's translation cited above. On the institutions of the Anglo-Saxon and related peoples, see Gummere, *Germanic Origins* (N. Y., Scribner's, 1892), now unfortunately hard to obtain. Bibliographical guidance to works of the Anglo-Saxon period will be found in H. M. Ayres's *Bibliographical Sketch of Anglo-Saxon Literature* (N. Y., Lemcke and Buechner, 1910).

Good critical editions of the Anglo-Saxon text are those by Wyatt and Chambers (Cambridge, Eng., second edition, 1920) and by W. J. Sedgefield (Manchester, Eng., second edition, 1913). The edition by F. Klaeber (Heath, 1922) contains a remarkable amount of information in condensed form.

III. The Song of Roland. A convenient and inexpensive translation into English prose is that by Miss Isabel Butler in the *Riverside Literature Series* (Houghton, Mifflin). The poem has been translated into English verse by Bacon (Yale University Press, 1914). The rendering in modern French prose by J. Geddes (Macmillan, 1906) contains a useful bibliography and an elaborate introduction, which will put the student in possession of the main facts in regard to the history and the interpretation of the poem, and will suggest the best sources for further reading. A useful survey of the Charlemagne romances is provided by Miss Jessie L. Weston's *The Romance Cycle of Charlemagne and his Peers*, in *Popular Studies in Mythology, Romance, and Folklore*, No. 10 (London, Nutt).

Convenient and reliable editions of the original Old French text are those by Clédat (Paris, Garnier, 1893), and by L. Gautier (Tours, Alfred Mame), the latter with a translation into modern French opposite the original, and introduction, notes, and glossary. For beginning a study of the Old French text the little volume by G. Paris, *Extraits de la Chanson de Roland* (Paris, Hachette), may be recommended. The more advanced student should not neglect the brilliant and important studies by J. Bédier, *Les Légendes Épiques*, 4 vols. (Paris, 1908, etc.).

IV. The Arthurian Romances. In general, consult W. Lewis Jones, *King Arthur in History and Legend* (Cambridge, Eng., 1911), a very useful brief summary; Howard Maynadier, *The Arthur of the English Poets* (Houghton, Mifflin, 1907); Jessie L. Weston, *King Arthur and His Knights, a*

Survey of Arthurian Romance, No. 4 of the *Popular Studies* (London, Nutt) ; and *Celtic and Medieval Romance* by A. Nutt, No. 1 of the *Popular Studies*. J. D. Bruce, *Evolution of the Arthurian Romances from the Beginnings down to the year 1300*, 2 vols. (Göttingen, 1923), may be used with profit by elementary students, though much in its pages is designed only for specialists. For the social background, consult L. Gautier, *La Chevalerie* (Paris, 1884) also in translation by Firth (London, 1891) ; and F. W. Cornish, *Chivalry* (New York, 1911). The 'Erec' and other romances of Chrétien have been translated into prose by W. W. Comfort in *Everyman's Library*, under the title *Eric and Enid*. A convenient translation of Geoffrey of Monmouth and other early chroniclers will be found in Giles's *Six Old English Chronicles* (Bohn Library). For a paraphrase of selections from Chrétien's romances, see W. W. Newell, *King Arthur and the Table Round*, 2 vols. (Houghton, Mifflin, 1898). The *Mabinogion* may be read in the admirable translation of Lady Charlotte Guest, in the edition with explanatory material by Nutt (London, Nutt, 1902), or in the cheaper edition, without Nutt's notes, in *Everyman's Library* (Dutton). For *Aucassin and Nicolete*, see Andrew Lang's exquisite rendering (N. Y., 1904). The *Morte Darthur* of Malory is issued in one volume in the *Globe Edition* (Macmillan), and in two volumes in *Everyman's Library*. Miss S. F. Barrow's *The Medieval Society Romances* (N. Y., 1924) illustrates the reflection of medieval life in selected romances. There are selections from the *Morte Darthur* with a good introduction by Mead in the *Athenæum Press Series* (Ginn).

V. The Legend of the Holy Grail. The best short outline of the view of the development of the medieval Grail legend adopted in the present volume is that by Nutt, No. 14 of the *Popular Studies*, 1902 (see above). Nutt's larger work, *Studies on the Legend of the Holy Grail*, is rather elaborate for

the general reader (London, Nutt, 1888). See, in general,
Maynadier, *The Arthur of the English Poets* (see above),
pp. 106–152. Wolfram von Eschenbach's *Parzival* has been
translated into English verse by Miss Jessie L. Weston, 2 vols.
(Nutt, 1894). On the Crusades, see Archer and Kingsford,
The Crusades (Putnam, 1910). A translation of Villehar-
douin's and of Joinville's memoirs is published in *Everyman's
Library* (Dutton). Miss Weston's *The Quest of the Holy
Grail* (London, 1913) affords a review of some of the problems
of the Grail legends, and sets forth her " nature-ritual "
theory in some detail. Miss L. A. Fisher's *The Mystic
Vision* (New York, 1917) stresses ecclesiastical influences.

VI. Reynard the Fox. A retelling of the story in English
prose by Joseph Jacobs appears in the *Home Library* (N. Y.,
A. L. Burt and Co.). There is a rendering in English verse
by F. S. Ellis, *The History of Reynard the Fox* (London, Nutt,
1894). The prose version by William Caxton has been edited
by Arber for the *English Scholar's Library* (London, 1878).
It may also be found in W. J. Thoms' *Early English Prose
Romances* (Routledge). For the original Old French text of
the *Roman de Renart* see the edition by E. Martin, 3 vols.
(Strasbourg and Paris, 1882–1887). For a paraphrase of the
Roman in modern French, consult Potvin, *Le Roman du
Renard, mis en vers, précédé d'une introduction et d'une biblio-
graphie* (Paris and Brussels, 1861). For general observations,
the discussion by M. Sudre, in the second volume of Petit
de Julleville's *Histoire* (see above) will be found excellent.

VII. The Ballads of Robin Hood. The standard collection
of the English and Scottish ballads is that edited by Child
(Houghton, Mifflin, 1882–1898), 5 vols., with elaborate intro-
ductions, variant versions, etc. The smaller edition on the
basis of this collection by Sargent and Kittredge (Houghton,
Mifflin, 1904) forms a convenient volume for the student.
The *Selections* edited by F. B. Gummere in the *Athenæum*

Press Series (Ginn) is provided with an excellent introduction
and notes. For a still more extended discussion of ballads
and ballad-problems, see Gummere's *The Popular Ballad*
(Houghton, Mifflin, 1907) — especially pp. 266–285 for Robin
Hood; and W. H. Clawson, *The Gest of Robin Hood* (*University of Toronto Studies*, Toronto, 1909).

VIII. The Canterbury Tales. The standard edition of the
complete works of Chaucer is that by Skeat in seven volumes
— the seventh containing miscellaneous pieces not by Chaucer (Oxford, Clarendon Press, 1900). The one-volume *Students' Edition* of the complete works by Skeat (Clarendon
Press), and the somewhat similar *Globe Edition* prepared by
Pollard and others (Macmillan), may be recommended. The
Canterbury Tales are issued separately in clearer type, and
with brief notes at the bottom of the page in a two-volume
edition by Pollard (Macmillan, 1894). H. N. MacCracken's
The College Chaucer (New Haven, 1913) contains a large
amount of text, with brief grammatical appendix and vocab-
ulary. For those who wish an introduction to the language,
versification, etc., of the *Tales* the edition of the *Prolog,
Knight's Tale,* and *Nun's Priest's Tale* by Liddell (Mac-
millan) will be found useful. Briefer introductory material
for these three texts is provided in the editions of Morris and
Skeat (Clarendon Press) and Mather (Houghton, Mifflin).
The best manual for the general student is Root's *Poetry of
Chaucer* (Houghton, Mifflin, revised edition, 1922). The
Chaucer-Bibliography by Miss Eleanor P. Hammond (Mac-
millan, 1908) is indispensable for any detailed study. G. G.
Coulton's *Chaucer and his England* (Putnam, 1908) and
Jusserand's *English Wayfaring Life in the Fourteenth Century*
(London, Unwin, 1901) give a good idea of the manners and
customs of the day. G. L. Kittredge's *Chaucer and His
Poetry* (Cambridge, Mass., 1915) is a delightful and stimu-
lating book.

INDEX

233

D